PSYCHE'S SISTERS

OTHER BOOKS BY CHRISTINE DOWNING:

The Goddess
Journey through Menopause
Face to Face to Face (coauthor)

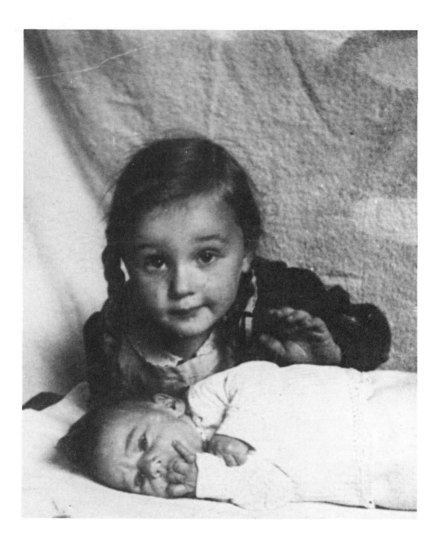

PSYCHE'S SISTERS

ReImagining
the Meaning of Sisterhood

CHRISTINE DOWNING

1817

Harper & Row, Publishers, San Francisco

Cambridge, Hagerstown, New York, Philadelphia, Washington
London, Mexico city, São Paulo, Singapore, Sydney

For Nancy
1937–1982
In Remembrance

Contents

List of Illustrations

FRONTISPIECE
The author and her sister, c. 1935, courtesy of Christine Downing.

INTRODUCTION
"Jungle Tales," by J. J. Shannon, courtesy of the Metropolitan Museum of Art, New York.

I: MYTHOLOGY'S SISTERS
"Isis and Nepthys," from the tomb of Nefretiri in the Valley of Queens. Photo courtesy of Christine Downing.

II. PSYCHOLOGY'S SISTERS
"Elektra at Agamemnon's Grave," from a Greek red-figure vase. Used with permission of the Musée du Louvre, Paris.

CONCLUSION
"Two Women Gossiping," from a Greek terracotta group sculpture. Used with permission of the British Museum, London.

Acknowledgments

I should like to thank my sister, my mother, my aunt, and my daughter, from whom I have learned so much of what I know about sisterhood.

I should also like to thank the women who have "sistered" me through the years devoted to the preparation of this book, especially Karen Brown, Carol Christ, Jan Clanton Collins, Adria Evans, Gail Hornstein, Puanani Harvcy, Elizabeth Keiser, Estella Lauter, Christine Osterloh, Margaret Pavel, Sabine Scheffler, Ruth Rusca, Suzanne Valery, and, most importantly, River Malcolm.

I want to thank Frank Oveis without whose persistent and loving prodding this book would still not be completed and George Lawler whose editorial "midwifery" and enthusiastic encouragement of my work has helped me immeasurably. I am also appreciative of the helpfulness of Kandace Hawkinson and Kathryn Sweet of Harper & Row San Francisco during the final stages of the book's production.

Our administrative assistant, Elaine Estwick, my department chair, Alan Sparks, and my dean, Marilyn Boxer, have all gone out of their way to support the writing of this book. Work on the project was supported in part by grants form the National Endowment for the Humanities and from the San Diego State Foundation.

INTRODUCTION

I feel the separateness
of cells in us, split-second choice

of one ovum for one sperm?
We have seized different
weapons

our hair has fallen long
or short at different times

words flash from you I never
thought of
we are translations into different
  dialects

of a text still being written
in the original

—Adrienne Rich

1. The Mysteries of Sisterhood

Shortly after completing my book on the relevance of Greek goddess traditions to the self-understanding of contemporary women,[1] I realized that there was one central relationship that I had neglected, the bond between sisters. I thought once again about the dream that had inspired that book and became aware that I had not yet exhausted the dream's meaning. In that dream I had found myself in a dark underground cave permeated with Her presence. Long after my eyes should have become accustomed to the darkness, I could, however, still not see Her, could still not discern Her shape. On waking, I remembered how often in my childhood my mother had told me that because I was born on the first day of spring I had a special relation to the Greek goddess of spring, Persephone. Thus it seemed natural that I should first identify the invisible She of the dream with Persephone and eventually discover that the other Greek goddesses were also manifestations of Her.

The engagements with these divine figures were transformative, yet my need to go in search of Her was not put to rest by them. The dream still haunted me. In the intervening years it has become more evident that She is not only goddess but *woman*—myself, of course, but at least as importantly other women, the actual other women whose lives intersect with mine. To know Her is to see us in our variegated individuality, to acknowledge how our interactions with one another reveal our gifts and our needs, our power and our frailty, our beauty and our ugliness, our compassion and our cruelty. To know Her is to know Her as Sister.

The discovery of the importance of sisterhood has led me to a new appreciation of the familiar tale about Eros and Psyche, in which, I have come to see, it is the interactions among sisters that instigate the heroine's journey toward self, toward *psyche*. This story in no way sentimentalizes sisterhood: Psyche's sisters are envious and cruel—but they push her in the way her soul requires (whereas Eros would happily have kept her in the dark). I have come to see Psyche's sisters as initiating us into an appreciation of how our sisterly relationships challenge and nurture us, even as we sometimes disappoint and betray one another.

Although feminism made us all newly aware of the importance of sisterhood, there was early on a tendency to conceive the sister bond only metaphorically and thus in highly idealized terms. Almost inevitably we then found ourselves subject to intense feelings of disillusionment when our "sisters" failed us, when we discovered that relationships between women can be as difficult, as demanding, as ineluctably ambivalent as all other human bonds. Returning to the source of the metaphor, the relation between actual biological sisters, may help us recover a more resilient and more complex sense of what sisterhood might mean. Because once seen this seems so obvious, I am intrigued by how rarely such a return has been envisaged.

The reengagement with the actual sister of our early years is only the beginning; it leads into an exploration of the ongoing meaning of that relationship throughout our lives, toward an understanding of how it reappears, transformed, in many of our friendships and love affairs, and to a deeply challenging revisioning of our innermost self.

Only gradually did I fully apprehend how much is changed if we free ourselves from the notion that the relation of mother to child is the paradigmatic human relation and set next to it as equally significant the relation of sibling to sibling. I now see such a shift of emphasis as affecting even how we construe our relationship to the other forms of life with which we share this planet. If instead of looking to the earth as Mother, as a mother on whom we are utterly dependent or from whom we must entirely free ourselves, we were to acknowledge the other two-legged and four-legged creatures, the creatures that crawl and swim and fly, as our brothers and sisters, we might yet be able to find ways of living with them before we destroy them and ourselves.

But that vision belongs at the end of this exploration. It has meaning only in the context of a more adequate understanding of sibling relationships than our culture immediately provides.

I came to it only by way of reengagement with the meaning of sisterly experience in my own life and with the meanings attached to it by folktale and myth and by depth psychology.

The awakening of my interest in sister-sister relationships was prompted by a variety of factors; suddenly the importance of these bonds became evident in my dreams, in my personal relationships, and in my scholarly work. It became clear that understanding these relationships implied consideration of the other modes of sibling interaction—the relationships between sisters and brothers and between brothers and brothers—as well. How else to be clear about what is peculiar to sisterly interaction and not true of all sibling bonds or of all same-sex sibling relationships? Certainly I had no intimation at the outset of how much—in my understanding of myself, of my relationships to women, of my work as teacher and therapist, of my sense of the interrelationship between the human and the natural world—would be transformed as I really came to appreciate the full significance of sister-sister bonding.

The personal imperative of a more honest engagement with sister-sister relationships was first announced by the frequent and insistent appearance of a particular dream motif: the task of recovering a lost sister. The dream sister combined, as dream figures so often do, memories associated with my familial sister, feelings aroused in contemporary relationships with close women friends, intimations concerning a neglected aspect of my inner life most appropriately represented in sister guise. The dreams seemed to imply that both the clarification of my bonds to women and the more solitary soul work involved going back to the beginning—to the sister with whom I shared my childhood.

Among my dreams one particularly stands out as embodying a great many of the aspects of the sister bond that were so persistently clamoring for attention:

A woman who is both my sister and my lover and I have been living together for a long while but realize that our relationship is in serious trouble and that we need help. We have heard of a woman who specializes in family repair work. She uses her own version of psychodrama that sounds somewhat like street theater, somewhat like television's "People's Court"—unconventional but reputedly effective.

We have tried other therapy without much success and are desperate.

We decide to try her. From the outside, her place looks like a shabby delicatessen in a seedy neighborhood. We are reminded of a storefront church or a fortune-teller's den. The room we enter is full of neighborhood types who appear at home in this setting but are not at all "our kind of people." We are nervous, not sure we belong or how well this approach is likely to work for us. Another couple is called on soon after we arrive. Everyone else, including us, sits and watches. Their work feels real and also productive. We are somewhat reassured (though we are puzzled by some half-heard mumblings about what good actors they are). The therapist is a middle-aged gypsylike woman. We discover that one of the men sitting in the "audience" with us is her husband. He is much older than she, a friendly, old-fashioned tobacco-chewing fellow. He chats with everyone in a way that provides a kind of running commentary on the therapy and seems to be responsible for keeping some kind of loose order among the observers. His presence, too, stimulates confidence.

Then is it our turn. My sister is called into the back room and soon appears "on stage." I recognize the scene she is reenacting immediately. The setting is the East Coast beach of our childhood summers. The scenery is stunningly convincing, as are the actors with whom she is playing in the sand. I am flooded with nostalgia, with memories of youthful happiness. Suddenly I realize that my sister is no longer visible. I do not see her on the beach or in the water. Her disappearance is frighteningly familiar. I feel compelled to jump into what I know is just a stage scene. The old man, the other spectators, sit unconcernedly in the shabby room, but I am very scared. I push my way onto the stage and discover how tawdry and ramshackle the setting actually is. But my sister has truly disappeared. There is a now-locked trapdoor on the stage floor through which she may have been pulled into some dark and fearsome basement. Desolate, afraid, horrified, I turn around to protest, but everyone has vanished, though the room and its furnishings are still intact.

I head for home, preparing to undertake the arduous, complicated task of recovering her. I am aware of feeling deeply betrayed because I now realize that the gypsy woman is really the uptown psychologist we have been going to for a long while who knows all our secrets. And the old man is her husband whom we often see just before or after our session and of whom we have become quite fond. He, too, knows a lot about us—funny, casual little details about our growing up, not important enough ever to have been brought up in therapy. All that both know is being used against us.

My sister, disappearing in the particular way that she has, seems all the more eerie because once long ago she and I had on the same night both dreamt of losing each other in just this way. Though we had never imagined it might actually happen, there is a strange fatedness about the use of so primal a fantasy to effect our separation. Yet despite everything, there is nothing hopeless about our situation; it is simply a difficult, deeply testing challenge. I somehow know that I will recover her, my sister, my lover—when I really understand it all.

The following night I dreamed of her again. This time my sister was being pursued and needed my help to disguise herself and then escape. When she left, I felt confident that she would get away safely and that we would eventually reconnect. What seemed most remarkable about the second dream was how I alternated between the two roles: at one moment I was deeply engaged in coming to my sister's aid, at the next I was myself the one who was being helped to escape. Within the dream this seemed completely natural.

In dream after dream she appeared, this figure who is both my literal sister and someone else, a more intimate presence in my contemporary life. We are together, we are separated; I search for her, I wait trustingly for her to find me. I am not sure who is who; we seem to be continually exchanging places, my sister and I: in my dreams so inextricably interconnected, in life so separate. She, the closest other in my life, and the most distant—so long neglected, she now insistently claimed my attention.

My memories of childhood are interfused with memories of her. I was four when she was born. I remember visiting my mother in the hospital and feeling awe at the little creature in her arms, more like me than any other being in the world—and yet utterly other. A photograph taken of us a few weeks later shows me looking down at her asleep in her crib and communicates my wonder. I remember how three months later the four of us, my mother and two-year-old brother, my sister and I, boarded the ship that would take us to America to rejoin our father, who (because of Hitler) had had to leave Germany just after she was conceived. I remember the reunion with him and how different his delight in her simply *being* felt from his pride in my courage and intelligence. I remember my mother reading to us from the book of German fairy tales she had brought across the ocean, holding my sister in her lap while I sat on the floor leaning against her knees. I remember teaching my sister to read almost as soon as I learned myself, so anxious was I to share the magic world of words with her. I remember wanting to grow up to be a writer and practicing by telling her stories every night after the lights went out, when we were supposed to be asleep. I remember winter weekends that my siblings and I spent practicing plays that I had made up, plays we performed for our parents late on Sunday afternoon. My sister was always the princess, the gift-child, the fairest in the land. I remember walking to and from school with her, two miles each way, I always at least three steps in the lead. I remember the family suppers at which each of us children would have a turn to tell about our day. I remember how she was always first and how endless her accounts would invariably be, beginning each time with her arriving at school, putting her books and lunchbox on her desk, hanging up her coat, tugging off her galoshes—detail after detail while I waited impatiently to tell of my own day's discoveries and triumphs.

The memories of childhood interactions come thick and fast and with them the feelings: my delight in her and my envy, my protectiveness and my bossiness, my admiration and my scorn, my joy in our intimacy and my sadness at how different we were. How surprisingly alive these feelings still are, how intense, how ambivalent.

In large measure I had worked through my relation to mother and father, to sons and daughter, to the man who was once my husband and is now my friend, and to my brother, but coming to terms with my sister's role in my life (and mine in hers) remained an outstanding challenge—a challenge, my dreams were suggesting, I could no longer evade. It was time, past time, for me to make sense and symbol of the sister bond.

Not only my dreams but events in outward life as well were conspiring to impress on me the timeliness of this particular sorting through. The first waking-life clue to the hazard of continuing to ignore any longer this neglected relationship had come a few years earlier when I thought that I might have uterine cancer. In the interval before I learned that there had been a misdiagnosis, it had become clear to me which of my friends I would call on for support. They were all sisterly figures, these imagined attendants—close women friends, a lover, my daughter—but my literal sister was not among them.

A year later my sister-in-law, a sister through all the years of my adult life, died. I felt that I who had always been the older sister, always the one to do everything first, now had a sister who had gone ahead of me. This sister, too, appears in my dreams. I remember one in which she is sister to her sister, nurses that sister through the difficult weeks and months of her dying and after her death learns: "This was the preparation; soon it will be your turn." I have come to understand how I, too, need my sister to prepare me for my death.

It seems not at all accidental that the need to come to a more conscious understanding of my relation to both my outer and my inner sister, to the personal sister and the archetypal one, appears just as I find myself in that phase of my life whose major task is preparation for death. That preparation, as I see it, is the soul work laid upon us when we have completed the passage through menopause. The themes of sisterhood and mortality are complexly interfused.

I believe this may be why the sorting through with the sister comes last—after all the other tasks. The objective is not patching-up, correction, or resolution; the task is reimagining, questioning, going deeper. It is an initiation into Hades, the realm where psyches live. The purpose is not primarily a better understanding of my past or our shared past, though that may be part of the way. The point, I came to recognize, would not be literal reconciliation with an estranged sister or, as I had at first imagined, the re-creation of a long-lost intense intimacy. It is not even primarily to help make me more capable in the present of giving and receiving love uncontaminated with unworked-through sister feeling—though that is very important to me. The pull to clarify the role of sisterhood in my life is certainly strengthened by my longing to love women (and especially the woman who is my mate) well. But the rediscovery of the sister is also a new and necessary discovery of self, and beyond that, it may be, as I have already intimated, an initiation into a new relationship to the earth herself, now perceived not as mother (as she so often is in mythology) but as sister, not simply as my source but as a being toward whom I have responsibility.

I do not mean to imply that the relation to the sister is important only in the last major life phase but that it is also, and perhaps especially, important then. The sister is present, at least implicitly, in every phase, not only at the beginning and the end.

> There were years you and I
> hardly spoke to each other
>
> we kept in touch, untouching
>
> lied about our lives
>
> We cleaved to each other across that space
>
> fingering webs
> of love and estrangement
>
> then one whole night
> our father dying upstairs
>
> we burned our childhood, reams of paper,
> till the birds sang
>
> Your face across a table now: dark
> with illumination
>
> This face I have watched changing
> for forty years
>
> has watched me changing[2]

There are particular times when the closeness or the distance becomes visible—as gift, as need, as curse—marriages, divorces, births, deaths. There are many times along the way when the pull to reconnect, to understand, becomes imperative. Yet my guess is that no matter how well or how poorly these earlier reencounters go, the sister bond will have to be reviewed again in this last life phase—even if we have decisively given it up as hopeless, even if it seems long ago successfully resolved.

Once my dreams and confrontations with death had impressed upon me the importance of the sister bond in my inner and outer life, it seemed self- evident. How could I have for so long ignored the determinative and unique role of same-sex sibling relationships?

For a woman the sister is the other most like ourselves of any creature in the world. She is of the same gender and generation, of the same biological and social heritage. We have the same parents; we grew up in the same family, were exposed to the same values, assumptions, patterns of interaction. (Of course, I know that the probability is that we share only half our genes and that no two children ever have quite the same parents—we experience them somewhat differently and evoke different responses from them. Nevertheless there is no other with whom we share so much.) The sibling relationship is among the most enduring of all human ties, beginning with birth and ending only with the death of one of the siblings. Although our culture seems to allow us the freedom to leave sibling relationships behind, to walk away from them, we tend to return to them in moments of celebration—marriages and births—as well as at times of crisis—divorces and deaths. At such moments we often discover to our surprise how quickly the patterns of childhood interaction and the intensity of childhood resentment and appreciation reappear.

Yet this other so like myself is, ineluctably, *other*. She, more than any other, serves as the one over against whom I define myself. (Research suggests that children are aware of the distinct otherness of siblings well before they have fully separated from the mother.) Likeness and difference, intimacy and otherness—neither can be overcome. That paradox, that tension, lies at the very heart of the relationship.

Same-sex siblings seem to be for one another, paradoxically, both ideal self and what Jung calls "shadow." They are engaged in a uniquely reciprocal, mutual process of self-definition. Although daughters create mothers as much as mothers create daughters, the relationship is not symmetrical as the one between sisters is. Of course, even between sisters there is some asymmetry, some hierarchy; birth order, relative age, does make a difference. But unlike the overwhelming, somehow sacred difference that separates mother and infant child, the differences between sisters are subtle, relative, on a profane scale.

The differences between siblings can be negotiated, worked on, redefined by the siblings themselves. The work of mutual self-definition seems typically to proceed by way of a polarization that half-consciously exaggerates perceived differences and divides up attributes between the sisters ("I'm the bright one, and she's the pretty one"). Often, too, sisters seem to divide up their parents between them ("I'm Daddy's girl, and you're Mommy's"). I am who she is not. She is both what I would most aspire to be but feel I never can be *and* what I am most proud *not* to be but fearful of becoming.

The sister is different from even the closest peer friend (though such a friend may often serve as a sister surrogate), for sisterhood is an ascribed not chosen relationship. We are stuck with our particular sister as we never are with a friend. John Bowlby says that the most important thing about siblings is their *familiarity*—siblings easily become secondary attachment figures to whom we turn when tired, hungry, ill, alarmed, or insecure. Siblings may also serve as playmates, but the role is different: we seek out a playmate when in good spirits and confident and what we want is, precisely, play. The relationship to a sibling is permanent, lifelong, one from which it is almost impossible entirely to disengage. (One can divorce a mate much more finally than a sibling.) Because that permanence helps make it the safest relationship in which to express hostility and aggression (safer than with our parents because we are never so dependent on a sibling as we are in infancy—and in imagination always—on our mother and father), the bond between same-sex siblings is very likely the most stressful, volatile, ambivalent one we will ever know.

I have discovered that the longing for relationship with the sister is felt even by women without biological sisters, and that all of us search for "her" in many surrogates throughout our lives.

The Sister and the Brother are what Jung would call archetypes, as present in our psychic life irrespective of literal experience as are the Mother or the Father. (It is easy for me to speak of "the" sister since I have only one. When there are several the archetype is likely to be divided among them in oft-shifting ways. Our relation to each has its own specific valence and significance, yet together they carry the complexity of the archetype.) Like all archetypes the Sister keeps reappearing in projected or "transference" form and has an inner aspect. Sorting through the meaning of sisterhood in our lives requires attending to all three modes: that of the literal sister(s), the surrogate sisters, and the sister within, the archetype.

I am who she is not. The inner sister—my ideal self and shadow self as strangely one—figures so significantly in the process of individuation that she is there whether I have a literal sister or not. Yet like all archetypes she demands actualization and particularization, demands to be brought into the outer world of distinct images. When there is no actual sister, there seem always to be imaginary sisters or surrogate sisters. Even when there is an actual sister, there are often fantasy figures or substitutes, as if the real sister were not quite adequate fully to carry the archetype, and yet the archetype needed nevertheless to be imaged, personified. The Sister appears with the particular face of a friend or a dream figure, of a character in a novel or a mythological heroine.

That the Sister is indeed one of those primal fantasies that Freud saw as active in our psychic life independent of historical experience has been confirmed for me by how frequently unsistered women have come to the workshops on sisters that I have led, knowing they, too, needed to work on the meaning of this relationship in their lives. The first time this happened, I wondered: "What do I have to say to them? What do I know of what it is like never to have had a biological sister?" Then I remembered: "Probably quite a bit." For I have a mother who was an only child and a daughter who has only brothers. My mother has told me how ardently she looked forward to my growing up, so that she might at last have a sister, and I know that as subtle counterpoint to the mother-daughter bond that relates me to my daughter there is a sister-sister one.

I realize also how my mother's understanding of sisterhood is colored by her not having had a sister as a child. She idealizes the relationship; she sees as sisterly only our intimacy not our rivalry; nor could she see anything of value in the stressful moments of interaction between my sister and myself when we were young. For over fifty years the encounters between her and her sister-in-law have been contaminated by a mutually obsessive jealousy, yet it would not occur to her that theirs is a sisterly relationship. My daughter's lack of a biological sister shows differently: since she grew up with brothers, men carry little mystery for her; she turns to women as lovers—and as sisters.

To call the Sister an archetype helps express my sense that there is a transpersonal, extrarational, *religious* dimension to sisterhood that endows all the actual figures upon whom we "transfer" the archetype with a numinously daemonic or divine aura. Yet I do not mean that there exists some universal, ahistorical essence of sisterhood. The trigger for an archetype is always particular experience; the degree to which such experiences are shared, recurrent, evocative of similar responses, is always to be explored not assumed. I have also been deeply impressed by Freud's observation that though we have made something sacred of parent–child love we have left that between brothers and sisters profane. I, too, experience the Sister archetype as less overwhelmingly numinous than that of the Mother. The Sister's sanctity is somehow commensurate with that which characterizes my own soul: she is woman not goddess. The engagement with mortal Psyche occurs in a different dimension from the one with Persephone, the goddess with whom I began my search of Her.

My particular interest lies with sister-sister relationships, but it seems obvious that fully to understand their uniqueness requires attending also to sister-brother and brother-brother relationships. I wanted to perceive more clearly how being a sister to a brother differs from sistering a sister. It seemed important to explore my intuition that brother-brother relations and sister-sister relations are not symmetrical. Because the first primary relationship in the lives of female children is to a same-sex other, the mother, same-sex bonding would, I suspected, have greater salience in the lives of women than in the lives of men, and sisters would figure more powerfully in women's psychology than brothers in men's.

When I first became aware of the archetypal character of the Sister I hoped to find a goddess who might model the role for me in all its complexity and depth. I sought a divine image who would represent the light and the dark aspects of what sisterhood encompasses. I remembered how, when I was ready to sort out the meaning of the other primary relationships in my life, a goddess had each time appeared as intercessor. Demeter and Persephone had helped me to clarify my relation to both my mother and my daughter, as Athene had served to illumine my father bond. Consideration of Hera's relation to Ares, Hephaistos, and Herakles had deepened my understanding of the relation between a mother and her sons, as Artemis's connection to Apollo had enhanced my appreciation of the sister-brother tie. Hera was there when it was time to attend to my relationship to my spouse. I had come to depend on the availability of such divine figures.

But I soon discovered that none of the Greek goddesses are in an intrinsic way paradigmatic of sister-sister bonding. It is true that Hestia, Demeter, and Hera are each daughter to Rhea and Kronos and that all three were swallowed by their father immediately after birth. Yet there are no mythological traditions about any interactions among them after their emergence from their father's stomach. That there are instead indications of cultic opposition (Demeter's temples are closed when Hera's are open), I take as a symbolic expression of how immersion in the patriarchal womb curtails or even destroys sisterly bonds.

The other major Olympian goddesses, Aphrodite, Artemis, Athene, even Persephone, have a common father, but that is so only in those later strata of the tradition where membership in the pantheon is defined in terms of relationship to all-father Zeus. Earlier mythological accounts represent Aphrodite as born of Ouranos' sea-tossed genitals and Zeus's fathering of Artemis and Persephone as ending with their conception: Leto is abandoned by Zeus long before her daughter is born, whereas Demeter deliberately shields her daughter from all paternal intervention. For Athene, on the other hand, Zeus's fatherhood is essential—she is his parthenogenetic daughter—but she has no mother. There is no indication of sisterly feeling among any of these goddesses, perhaps because (as Adrienne Rich suggests) it is the common bond to the mother that creates sisterhood and these divinities each have a different mother:

> The daughters never were
> true brides of the father
>
> the daughters were to begin with
> brides of the mother
>
> then brides of each other
> under a different law[3]

Regretfully I accepted that my exploration of sisterhood must be undertaken without the goddesses, at least without the Greek ones from whom I have learned so much. Then I discovered that there are nonetheless powerful paradigms of sister-sister bonding in Greek mythology—among the mortal women, the heroines of cult, epic poetry, and tragedy. Perhaps this acknowledges that we mortal women need one another for self-definition as goddesses do not. Goddesses are self-sufficient, complete in themselves, individuated. The various stages of their life— childhood, youth, maturity (as immortals they are immune to aging and death)—are eternally copresent. Their wholeness encompasses what in us is divided between the conscious and unconscious aspects of our being; there is no segregation of ego from ego-ideal or from shadow. What need have they of a sister?

Like ourselves, on the other hand, the mortal women in Greek mythology become themselves through engagement with others, through projection, differentiation, and reintegration, through struggle and suffering, love and hatred, failure and death. Among these mortal women sisterly bonds are intrinsically related to character and fate.

There are still disputes among scholars about whether these figures—Helen, for example, or Ariadne—were originally divinities who were at some point reduced to mortal status (perhaps in connection with the establishment of the Olympian pantheon) or were to begin with historical personages, later immortalized through poetry and cult. Yet, either way, the point is that they are mortal *and* archetypal. Their "immortality" (like that of their male counterparts) depends on their death. As Carl Kerenyi expresses this, "the glory of the divine" that falls on these figures is strangely combined with "the shadow of mortality":

The stress is laid on the human side in all its manifestations, not least in the burden of destiny and suffering which the heroes endure. With this manner of emphasizing the human element, the mythology of the heroes takes a new direction from the very beginning, which characteristically leads into Tragedy.[4]

The heroes and heroines are always in contact with death; death belongs to their "shape." They die and often lead others to their death. Their sanctuaries are tombs. Their cult is a cult of the dead. Their immortality is conferred by poetry and ritual, by culture, by human activity. Thus for these mortal heroines their death is to their immortality as nature is to culture.

That the two themes of mortality and sisterhood should in Greek mythology be so closely interwoven feels, in retrospect, so right as to be almost inevitable. In my life, too, as I have noted, these themes appeared together. Being fully human, being fully ourselves as *human* women, seems to require the refraction provided by a sisterly other. The exploration of sisterhood seems to lead toward a deeper understanding of human mortality and of the significance for the soul of the sometimes painful engagement with the real *otherness* of actual women.

Thus I came to discover that questioning the reasons for the absence of the sister bond from the Greek goddess traditions brought into view the intrinsic correlation between our sisteredness and our mortality. I learned that there *are* myths, though not where I had first looked for them. Nonetheless I was again disappointed to learn that the Greeks had no mysteries, no rituals, celebrating the tie of sister to sister as the Eleusinian mystery acknowledges the profound significance of the mother-daughter bond and as the cult of the Dioscuri honors the bond between brothers. The sister-sister relation was evidently more invisible to the Greeks than the maternal or fraternal one. Perhaps this is not surprising in a culture uncommonly comfortable with male-male bonding and perhaps unusually fearful of intimacy among females. Or it may be simply that the male poets and philosophers on whom our knowledge of classical Greece is so greatly dependent had no direct access to the relationship of woman to woman. To them the sister bond was of necessity obscure and mysterious.

I see it as my project to move from one sense of mystery to

the other; I believe it is time to bring sisterhood out of obscurity and honor it with the reverence due a sacred mystery.

To do so means beginning by trying to remember as concretely and sensuously as we can our earliest memories of interactions with our siblings and especially our sisters (or, failing such memories, our dearest childhood playmates or most important imaginary companions), as I began to do in the first pages of this chapter. We need to return to that place where memory and imagination flow together, to the time of beginnings. We need also to recall our dreams, the dreams in which our brothers, our sisters, appear—as they were then, as they are now, as they are only in dream.

We need, also, I believe, to look beyond our own memories to those of our shared heritage. Exploring what it might mean to pay due homage to the Sister has led me to attend to my own memories and dreams, to the events of long ago and of yesterday. It has meant listening to the confidences of others, given generously and spontaneously since I first announced my newly awakened interest. Another woman drawn to this theme might have made these contemporary reminiscences a more explicit focus of her study or might have given her attention to the scrutiny of famous historical sisterly pairs or the representations of sisterhood in modern literature.[5] What I felt pulled to do was to return to the images through which our culture has celebrated, remembered, imagined the sister bond. We need to peruse and muse over the images of folktale and myth—and over the representations provided by the mythologists of soul of our time, the depth psychologists. It is time to retell the familiar stories, to rediscover what we may already know without fully knowing that we know it—the many ways in which brotherhood and sisterhood have been lived and imagined in the past—so that we may reimagine sibling experience for ourselves with as much richness and depth as possible.

I
MYTHOLOGY'S SISTERS

When sisters separate they haunt each other
as she, who I might once have been, haunts me
or is it I who do the haunting

—Adrienne Rich

2. Fairy-Tale Sisters

When I first realized that Greek goddess traditions would be of little help in illuminating the meaning of sisterly experience, my immediate response was to turn to the German fairy tales with which I had grown up, tales in which I knew that sibling relationships were a pervasive theme. I suspect this is true in most folklore traditions, but for me the stories collected by the Grimm brothers define the genre. They have shaped my consciousness, perhaps more than is true for most American children. The scene of my immigrant mother gathering her children around her to read them the stories that connected her to her own German childhood is indelibly fixed in my memory. Children with different ethnic heritages may remember tales other than those that nurtured me, but in my case the turn to fairy tale is inevitably the turn to the Grimms' household tales.

These are the stories I heard with my brother and sister. Indeed, I am not sure which is more powerful—the way my experiences with my own siblings shaped my response to the tales or the way my sense of what it is to have a brother, to have a sister, was shaped by the tales. Margarethe von Trotta opens her stunning film *Sisters, or the Balance of Happiness* with a scene of two girls sitting listening to their mother read them a fairy tale about two sisters. We are shown how the older girl imagines the tale as one involving herself and her own younger sister. As the film unfolds we come to see how the tale's version of their relationship corresponds to the tragic tensions between the sisters years later. That sense of the shaping power of these tales rings true to me.

Freud helped me understand how memories of fairy tales may serve as screen memories of our own childhood. His case history "The Wolfman" revolves around the interpretation of a childhood dream in which the manifest images are clearly derived from an illustrated book of Russian folktales. His analysis seeks to determine whether the recovered memory evoked by the dream's interpretation is based on factual experience or on primal fantasy. What really happened in the patient's childhood? What was only imagined? There seems to be no certain way of deciding.[1]

There were times in my life, late adolescence, early adulthood, when I looked down on these tales simply because they were tales my mother told me. The periods of disparagement of her coincide with periods of seeing fairy tales as childish, oversimple, outgrown. Now I have come to value knowing myself as part of a chain of tellers that goes back through her to her mother and her mother's mother, a seemingly endless chain. I understand better how important it was for my mother, the young immigrant alone in a foreign land, to tell her children the stories she'd been told and thus to feel some continuity between our childhoods and her own.

As I return to these stories once again, I am surprised to discover how deeply imbedded in my psyche are their characters and plots. My identifications with Gretel and with Cinderella's older sisters are apparently even older than my identification with Persephone or Athene. I remember Thomas Mann's observing that although in the life of the race myth is early, in the life of the individual the interest in it comes late.[2] I suspect that in the life of the race fairy tales come late, but in the life of the individual early.

The Grimms themselves spoke of fairy tales as the remnants of old myths, the playful derivatives of an ancient intuitive vision of life and the world.[3] The lateness of fairy tales as compared to myths is confirmed by their abstractness, the ease with which they speak simply of *the* river or forest, *the* king or queen, the facility with which one can substitute the young maiden of one tale for the heroine of another. The relative youth of fairy tales is also manifest in their clear-cut morality, in their forthright acceptance of the status of a profane rather than a sacred role and in the insistence on a happy ending.[4]

But other characteristics suggest that they do connect us to an age-old wisdom, that they may preserve reminiscences of a mythological tradition older than the officially preserved one, reminders of a matrifocal culture. Indeed, I wonder if these tales may not more adequately represent the original myth-making impulse than do the official myths, which so often demand exact retelling or literal belief. Fairy tales celebrate the imagination of teller and listener. The genre's characteristics encourage imagining, reimagining. I remember, for example, how easily as a child listening to these tales *the* forest became the woods of our family's Saturday afternoon walks, *the* father my own. As an adult I have also learned how easily the spontaneous imaginative response is diminished if we get too involved in allegorical interpretation and look upon the tales as only illustrations of psychological truths we already know from elsewhere. This danger threatens Jungians as much as Freudians; little differentiates the search for animas from the search for vaginas.

Though students of the genre argue about whether fairy tales are really for children or really for adults,[5] I see them as being told for the sake of the relation between children and parents, childhood and adulthood. They are told in the parent-child context and about it. They are about the relation within us of child and adult throughout our lives. They are about growing up—which we never fully do, as we never fully leave behind the exaggerated feelings of childhood. Fairy tales are stories about the initiation into gendered adulthood, a transition not given in myths: gods and goddesses have childhoods and adulthoods, but they don't grow up; they exist eternally in both modes. Siblings play such a central role in fairy tales in part because of the role that sisters and brothers play in helping one another separate from their parents and grow up.

Within the family the teller of these tales is most typically the mother, as was true in my childhood home and again when I had children of my own. Remembering these tales when we are adults returns us to the early scenes in which she played the dominant role. So often *in* the tales as well, the central role is given to the mother—a vision of how things are that is congruent with the child's experience. The fairy-tale father is often well-meaning but ineffectual—think of Cinderella's father or of Snow White's. The ogre or giant is secretly but ridiculously vulnerable. Power lies with the mothers—ambivalent power. The benevolent fairy godmother is always balanced by the cruel and wicked stepmother; the two belong together.

The distinction in these tales between the good and the bad mother, the kind and the selfish daughter, is dramatically explicit—and this is often viewed as defect. Yet my memory of my own childhood response to these stories persuades me that they encourage a complex, not an over simple, understanding of the self. The stories serve to communicate the coexistence of a dark and a light side in oneself and in others. I remember so well how undeniably I recognized myself not simply in the well-favored protagonists but even more forcibly in Snow White's jealous stepmother and in Mother Holle's selfish daughter.

The plots feature female protagonists or a male seeking to win the king's daughter through whom alone he may have access to a throne. To judge the fairy-tale heroine as an advertisement for the virtues of feminine passivity (as some feminists have done)[6] is, it seems to me, to misjudge, to confuse receptivity, introversion, cooperation, an openness to intuitive wisdom, with inactivity and dependence. I see these tales as celebrating an animistic consciousness that assumes a relationship to the natural world characterized by interdependence rather than domination, that presents the relation between humans and animals as a relation between persons. The stories introduce us into an enchanted realm without the usual sharp distinction between the sacred and the profane. Magic enters the everyday world. Communion between humans and animals is possible. Metamorphoses occur; brothers become roebuck or swans; frogs or bears become princes. Fairy tales return us to a time "when wishing still helped," when we knew it is not always appropriate to rely on heroic willing, on *making* happen. So often in fairy tales the successful outcome depends on sorting through, on waiting for the right time, on being willing to be helped and to be helpful.

In folktales, as Geza Roheim noted, the ever-recurring theme is the triumph of Eros (whereas in myth it is Death that wins in the end).[7] Fairy tales are about love, the importance of overcoming narcissism, the primacy of relationship. The *telos* is marriage, which serves to represent the reconciliation in us of male and female, parent and child, sister and brother. The endings are directed toward generativity, toward the birth of the child— directed beyond the story, toward the retelling of the story.

The happy endings that characterize the genre are nonetheless not sentimental. Happiness is possible—in the tale—in fantasy. The happy ending is an act of grace, what Tolkien calls a "good catastrophe," a sudden joyous turning.[8] The fairy tale provides no guarantee of such an outcome—but it denies the universal finality of evil. If the sober realism of myth were the only truth, we might be led toward too fatalistic an acceptance of tragedy. Fairy tales remind us that the realm of magic is still accessible, that the silent may speak, the ugly may be transformed into the beautiful, the lonely into the loved.

When I glance at the table of contents of my copy of the Grimms' anthology, I am struck by how relatively few of those stories I really remember clearly and by how central to those I do recall is the theme of sibling interaction. As I return to these tales now I know I want to include not only those that focus on what happens between sisters but also those that represent brother-brother and sister-brother relationships. I am curious to discover how important gender is in folklore, how the difference between female and male is rendered, whether same-sex sibling interactions are perceived as intrinsically different from contra-sex ones.

An exploration of sister-sister relationships ideally begins with an examination of the traditions about brother-brother ties. We need to examine the depicted differences between brother-brother and sister-sister relationships and ask whether there are aspects traditionally identified with fraternal bonds that are more relevant to female experience than the fairy tales themselves admit. To dismiss these tales as irrelevant to us is to cut ourselves off from an invaluable resource. For these tales where the autonomous existence of the siblings is taken for granted, where rivalry is assumed, where competition is directly and actively expressed, are in fact about dimensions of sibling experience not at all peculiar to brothers.

I imagine that the many stories that focus on brother-brother relationships were relatively rarely retold in a family with two daughters and but one son; certainly I remember them less clearly than the tales of sister-brother or sister-sister interaction.

But I have come to believe that these tales, too, are relevant to a woman's understanding of sibling experience and to a full appreciation of how brotherhood and sisterhood compare to one another. We might even find that sometimes brothers care for one another in "sisterly" ways or that sisters compete in a way we had imagined specific to brothers.

As I reread the stories about fraternal bonds, I discover how often in these stories there are three brothers, all engaged by the same challenge or all courting the same royal maiden. The youngest succeeds where the older brothers fail, because he is less self-confident and less self-reliant, because he is patient and modest, willing to be helped, willing to be helpful.

In "The Queen Bee," the youngest, "who was called Simpleton," dissuades his more violent brothers from destroying an anthill just for the fun of it, from killing two ducks for their supper, from building a fire that would force some bees to leave their honey-filled nest. Later the ants help him recover a princess's thousand pearls, the ducks help him retrieve the key to the princess's bedchamber from the bottom of the lake, and the bees help him distinguish which of the king's three daughters had eaten a spoonful of honey before she fell asleep. She, of course, is the youngest, the fairest, and her father's favorite. Simpleton marries her and eventually succeeds to his throne. His brothers, relying only on themselves, fail at the very first task and are turned to stone—though at the end of the tale they return to their natural form and marry the two elder daughters.

In "The Three Feathers" the youngest brother is again called Simpleton. In this tale a king announces that the one among his three sons who brings him the most beautiful carpet will be heir to the kingdom. The father blows three feathers in the air; the oldest brother is to follow the first feather, which flies toward the east; the second follows the westward flying feather. But Simpleton's feather flies straight up and then falls to the ground. At first downcast and resigned to failure, he then notices that beside the fallen feather there is a trapdoor. He raises the door and goes down into an underworld where a family of toads comes to his aid and provides him with a stunningly beautiful carpet. Though he has clearly won, the two older brothers persuade their father that Simpleton is just not bright enough to inherit the throne. Twice more the father announces a challenge and blows three feathers into the air; twice more Simpleton wins by descending into the earth and asking the toads for help. Only then is the brothers' opposition put to rest.

Both tales posit rivalry between brothers as a given; both suggest that violence, braggardly self-assertion, extroverted staying-on-the-surface, are self-defeating. The youngest brother is the one able to fulfill the tasks, the others are represented as ultimately reconciled to his victory. I sense that not only in the fairy tales but in our own lives, rivalry between sisters is less often acceptable, less often consciously acknowledged, and so less often worked through and resolved. I am also struck by how often it is the youngest, most "feminine" brother who is able to succeed in a way that dissolves the corrosive competition with which brother-brother tales begin. The youngest brother, strangely, has access to a "femininity" that *we* women often have difficulty accessing when engaged in our more surreptitious struggles with our sisters!

The most interesting tale about brotherly interaction in the Grimms' collection is the long, involved one called "The Two Brothers." It opens by telling us that once upon a time there were two brothers, one rich and evil-hearted, the other poor but good. The focus of the story, however, is on the poor brother's twin sons, who to begin with are "as like to each other as two drops of water." On reaching adulthood, they realize they must separate. Vowing to love each other always, they stick a magical knife into a tree at the place where they part. The knife will enable each to check on the other's fate: the side of the knife turned in the direction taken by each brother will remain bright as long as he's alive but will rust if he dies. During the course of his journey the younger of the two comes to a town decked in mourning. He kills the dragon that has laid waste to the countryside and rescues the king's daughter destined to be sacrificed to the beast. As he and the beautiful maiden, faint and weary from this adventure, lie down to rest before returning to her father's castle, another soldier comes upon them. He chops off our hero's head, seizes the maiden in his arms, gathers up the hacked-up bits of dragon, and persuades the king that he is the dragonslayer. But animals whom the brother had much earlier befriended put his head back on his body and restore him to life—and on the very day when the princess is due to be married to the false suitor, the true one returns and persuades the king that he is the rightful bridegroom. The two are married and live in happiness together.

But the story is not yet over. One day out on a hunt, the young king cannot resist pursuing a lovely snow white hind that leads him deep into a haunted wood. There he comes upon a witch who turns him into stone. At this point the other brother (whose life in the meanwhile has consisted only in aimless and fruitless wandering) reenters the tale. He has an intuition that it is time to go look at the knife they had stuck into the tree and learn how his brother is doing. Finding his brother's side of the knife half-bright, half-rusted, he hopes it is not too late to save him. When he arrives at his brother's castle, he is taken for the young king. Thinking the confusion may help him in his mission, he even allows himself to be taken to the young queen's bed, though he carefully lays a two-edged sword between them. When he learns of his brother's venture into the enchanted forest, he decides to go in search of him. He, too, follows the beautiful hind deep into the woods and meets the wicked witch. But this brother is immediately suspicious of her and threatens her until she leads him to his brother. She then touches the stone figure with her wand and returns him to life. The reunion between the two brothers is joyful, until the older one carelessly jokes about having been welcomed into the young queen's bed. The other in a fit of jealous rage strikes off his brother's head—and immediately repents. Luckily, the helpful animals are again able to replace the head and restore life, and the two proceed together back toward the palace. Even the bride cannot tell them apart, until she remembers a talisman she had given her husband. In outward appearance the brothers are still indistinguishable, although very different in character—one reckless and brave, the other so feckless but loyal. The story celebrates their reunion and their complementarity; they are, indeed, two sides of one knife.

As I reflect on these tales about brothers I discover more relevance in them to my own experience than I might have anticipated. Sisters, too, can be rivals, though it often seems that it is less easy for us to admit that as a given, to enjoy it as a challenge. Is there something about sisterly intimacy that makes overt competition more frightening, less acceptable? Is the rivalry thereby less likely to be worked through to resolution and restored harmony? In these tales about brothers the ambivalence seems to be sorted out on a temporal plane: first there is conflict, then resolution. I am struck, too, by how these fraternal interactions take place in the sphere of action, in the outer world, not in the realm of feeling. The brotherly aspect of sibling experience (whether it's that of males or females) seems to pertain to this outer dimension, to a world in which we are clearly distinct persons, where our polar differences are discovered to be complementaries. The separateness of these brothers seems to be a given; what needs to be learned is their interdependence, that each is helper and helped. In a sense this feels to me like the *easy* part of sibling experience. I believe it is a part that brothers live more readily than sisters. I can remember watching my four sons struggle with one another while they were young and realizing how different their conflicts were from those between my sister and myself. And while I envied their open and overt resolution of competitiveness, I sensed how little they knew of what is most rich about sister-sister relationships.

My memory of some of the stories about brothers and sisters is vivid, especially stories like "Hansel and Gretel" that idealize the relationship and see the sister and brother as mutually helpful and supportive—though I find that in the version of these tales I carry around in my head the role of the sister is often more emphasized than in the Grimms' renditions! In "Hansel and Gretel," for instance, when the two children find themselves abandoned by their desperately poor parents, Hans is at first the resourceful one who scatters the white pebbles that allow them to retrace their way home by moonlight and who the second time they are taken to the woods makes little balls of the bread the mother has given him, hoping they might serve the same purpose. I had always thought it was Gretel who had thus tried to assure their safe return. Indeed, I wonder even now if my mother, telling the story to an older sister (me) and her younger brother may not have *told* it that way! In either case, the plan doesn't work, for the birds eat the bread morsels and the children are lost in the woods. A bird leads them to the gingerbread house, to the apparently all-giving mother who turns out to be a witch. The witch locks Hans in a cage and begins to fatten him up as a succulent feast for herself. Now it is, even in the written version, time for Gretel to play rescuer. When the witch asks the girl to light the oven in which she plans to roast Hans, Gretel pleads ignorance and persuades the witch to show her how. Quickly the girl pushes the witch into the oven where she is burnt to death. Gretel releases Hans, and the two start toward home. After two hours of walking they come to a great stretch of water. Hans despairs, "The river's too wide, there's no bridge; we'll never get across." But Gretel sees a duck that she is confident will help them. Sure enough, the duck carries them on her back, one after the other, and the children succeed in finding their way home.

The tale called "Brother and Sister" is again a story of two children who find themselves alone against unloving parents. Again, each has a chance to play the role of helper. It is the brother who knows they must leave, but the sister who heeds the warning that the brooks in the forest turn those who sip from them into wild beasts. Twice she is able to persuade her brother not to drink, but the third time his thirst is too much for him and he cannot refrain. As soon as the first drops touch his lips, he is transformed into a roebuck. The sister finds a little hut in which they can live and promises never to leave him. Each day she gathers tender grass to feed him; each night she sleeps with his back as her pillow. One day as they hear the horns of the king's huntsmen, the roebuck cannot bear not to join the hunt. Reluctantly, the sister opens the door, and the lovely animal joyfully bounds off. One of the huntsmen follows him home in the evening and hears him call, "Little sister, let me in." The next evening the king himself comes to the hut and calls out, "Little sister, let me in." Of course, he finds the maiden beautiful and takes her home and marries her. The roebuck comes along and is given the run of the palace garden. But when the wicked stepmother from whom the brother and sister had fled at the beginning of the tale learns of their good fortune, she determines to spoil it. Shortly after the young queen gives birth to a son, the stepmother, disguised as a chambermaid, kills the new mother and puts her own daughter in the queen's bed. The king is evidently as impetuous and blind as the brother; he is off hunting when his young bride is due to give birth and doesn't seem to notice that his beautiful bride has been replaced by a one-eyed imposter. But every night the true queen comes into the nursery and breast-feeds her child. The nurse, who discovers these nightly visits, finally has the courage to tell the king. The next midnight he waits in the nursery, recognizes his true wife, and she is restored to life. The witch and her daughter are killed, and the roebuck is restored to his human form. The tale ends: "And so the sister and brother lived happily together all their lives." Their relationship, not the sister's to her husband or her child, is the point of the story.

Another brother-sister tale is "The Juniper Tree." Here a first wife dies giving birth to a son; the second wife fears this boy, her stepson, will deprive her own daughter of any inheritance. One day, in a fit of jealous rage, she kills the little boy and then rearranges things so that her own daughter, who adores the boy, believes she is responsible. The mother then tells her daughter they must let no one know of the death. She chops the little boy into pieces and mixes the morsels into a delicious black-pudding, which she then serves to the father. The daughter weeps through the cooking and through the eating but says nothing. At the end of the meal she gathers up the boy's bones in a handkerchief and carries them out to the juniper tree in their front yard. As she lies under the tree, she hears a bird sing and then sees it fly away; the handkerchief with the bones has disappeared. Later the bird returns, singing, "My mother she killed me; my father he ate me; my sister gathered together all my bones." The mother, curious about the strange song, comes out of the house to hear it more clearly. The bird drops a millstone on her head and kills her. The brother is returned to his own shape, and he and his sister and their father are joyfully reunited.

These representations of brother-sister relationship suggest a mutuality of devotion and concern; each in turn plays the role of rescuer. This is certainly a pattern I recognize as true of my own actual connection to my brother in adulthood as well as in childhood. Especially in the years since his wife's death, I have seen us turn to each other for a support available without question and accessible nowhere else. After years of relatively little intimacy, the trust in each other established in childhood was effortlessly at our disposal again. Perhaps there is some "mothering" in the sister's nurturance, some "fathering" in the brother's support, but more often the mode of caring seems almost independent of gender, as though there were some generically *sibling* form of love. The intense ambivalence that characterizes both child-parent relationships and same-sex sibling relationships is more muted here. The pattern seems to be that the opposition, the challenge, the turmoil comes from the outside world, the help from within the relationship. I understand this to have an inner significance as well: these stories point to an inner resource of energies and perspectives, complementary to our everyday version of ourself, that we can draw upon in situations of need; this inner resource is very different from that provided by an inner father (who might demand full maturity and mastery) or mother (who might offer complete exoneration and forgiveness). The inner brother or sister, as imagined in the fairy tales, honors our humanness, helps without asking too much or giving too much.

There is another fairy-tale version of brother-sister relationship more distant from my own experience. In this pattern the sister is represented as the rescuer of a group of brothers, of twelve brothers or seven ravens or six swans. Of course these stories make me think of my one daughter and her four brothers, but I don't actually find much connection—my daughter does not seem to be *that* kind of sister. These stories, more than the others, seem reflective of how brothers might view a sister; they yield less to an examination from the female perspective. Yet both Freud and the Jungian scholar Marie Louise von Franz view them as among the most psychologically significant of all fairy tales.

In the story "The Twelve Brothers" a king and queen who have twelve sons are expecting another child. The king decides that if this child is a girl, the boys must die in order that the daughter might inherit the entire kingdom. The mother warns the sons, who run away into the forest. When the girl is ten years old, she notices twelve men's shirts among the laundry and learns about her brothers. She sets out in search of them and soon finds their hut. She and the youngest brother embrace and weep with joy, until he remembers the agreement among the brothers that, in revenge for having been threatened with death on account of a girl, they will kill any girl they meet. She tells him, "I will willingly die, if by so doing I can save my brothers," but once the other brothers learn who she is, they welcome her and all thirteen live together in harmony. But one day, wishing to gather a pretty bouquet for their supper table, she picks twelve lilies growing in the garden. At that instant the brothers are turned into swans, the hut and garden disappear, and the girl finds herself quite along in the wild wood. An old woman tells her that the only way she can save her brothers is by being absolutely silent for seven years. A king comes by, and taken by her beauty, asks her to marry him. She nods in agreement, and he takes her home. They live happily together, though she never speaks or smiles. Eventually the king's jealous mother persuades him that his ever-silent bride must be a witch, and he sentences her to death. Of course she does not speak in her own behalf, and so, with tears in his eyes, the still-loving king has her tied to the stake and orders the great fire to be lit. At that moment the seven years are up, the ravens appear in the sky, touch ground, are transformed back into men, and rescue their sister. Now she can persuade the king of her innocence, and all, king and sister and brothers, live together in harmony until their death.

The story of "The Seven Ravens" is much the same. This time a father with seven sons finally has a daughter, though the child is so weak it is feared she will die. The father sends the sons to get water for a hurriedly arranged baptism. They inadvertently break the water jug and are afraid to return. The worried and impatient father cries out, "I wish they'd all turn to ravens" and—since this is a fairy tale—they do. Both parents regret what has happened but cannot undo it; they comfort themselves with the daughter, who soon grows strong and beautiful. On growing up she, too, learns of her brothers and their fate; feeling responsible, she decides she must somehow effect their rescue. Her search for them takes her to the very end of the world. Neither sun nor moon will help her, but the morning star tells her that her brothers are imprisoned within a glass mountain and gives her a chicken bone that will open it to her. She loses the bone but cuts off one of her own fingers and, using it as a key, succeeds in opening the door of the mountain and freeing her brothers.

In a third variant of this motif, the story called "The Six Swans," a widowed king has seven children, six sons and a daughter, whom he loves more than anything else in the world. He is tricked into remarriage with a beautiful but witchlike wife. Fearing she might harm the children, he hides them in a lonely castle deep in the forest. But, of course, she eventually learns of these children whom the king can't resist visiting and discovers the secret way to their hiding place. With her own hands she makes six little shirts of white silk and sews a magic charm into each. She then makes her way into the forest, finds the boys, and throws the shirts over them. They are forthwith changed into swans. The girl is saved because the queen does not know of her existence. Setting out in search of her lost brothers, the sister finds a little hut with six little beds. At dusk there is a great whirring of wings as six swans come flying in the window, quickly shed their feathers, and are revealed as her brothers. They tell her they can reassume their human form but for fifteen minutes each evening. Only if she were to remain resolutely silent for six entire years and during that period were to sew them six shirts of starwort could they ever be set free permanently. Of course, she resolves to deliver her brothers. Again a king out on a hunt finds the maiden and, though she remains mute, falls deeply in love with her and takes her home as his bride. Again his mother is wicked and jealous and from the very beginning seeks to slander the strangely silent bride. When a child is born, the old queen steals it away, smears the sister's mouth with blood and accuses her of being a man-eater. She says nothing in her own defense but resolutely keeps sewing at the shirts. The king loves her and trusts her, but when her second and third children also disappear and she still will not explain the blood on her lips, the king agrees he must have her burnt as a witch. Again the day scheduled for the sentence to be carried out is the one that marks the end of the six years. As she waits at the stake holding the six shirts, all finished except for the left sleeve of the last one, the swans come flying by. She throws the shirts over them, they become again her handsome brothers, and she is saved. The wicked old queen is killed in her stead, and the king, the queen, and her six brothers live many years in happiness and peace.

Von Franz sees the rescuing silence of the sister in these tales as signifying a deeply introverted attitude that protects the growth of the unconscious. The sisters, she says, represent the anima that makes possible the male's return from bewitchment by the instinctual to the realm of human relationship. Thus von Franz accepts the happy ending of these stories as signifying real progress in the individuation process (though she is less sanguine about "The Seven Ravens" tale.)[9] Freud, too, was intrigued by the motif of the silent sister, whom he identifies with the ancient goddess of death. He reminds us that the brothers are initially threatened with death because of their sister's very existence and it is because of her that they are transformed into swans or ravens—but it is also she who rescues them. Freud sees these stories as illustrating our longing to turn the sister who represents death into the one who rescues us from death, as thus expressing our deep wish to deny our mortality. He understands these tales to be about the male task of accepting femininity and finitude. Men's relation to the feminine, to the denied feminine aspects of their own psyche, is a relation to passivity, vulnerability, and morality. The stories see—and evade— this deep lesson.[10] Both von Franz and Freud interpret this group of tales from the perspective of male psychology. My sense is that for a man the sister may carry psychological significance that only a sister can carry for a woman. Sibling experience is not symmetrical, the stories suggest: sisters may carry a more profound meaning for brothers than brothers can for sisters. Given that primary connection to the mother, contrasexuality may inevitably be more important in the psychology of men than in that of women. For women, same-sex experience may be more important.

With respect to sister-sister relationships, fairy tales again seem to have two ever-repeating plots, the polarity plot and the complementarity plot. In the first we are given sisters who are opposite to one another in both fate and character: a good but unfortunate sister and her evil but more fortunate sister(s). The plot is one of simple reversal, so that by the end of the tale the good sister is now also the blessed one and the evil are cursed. In these tales the rivalry is often presented as taking place between *step*sisters—in fairy tales the "step" relation often serves to designate the evil side of the feminine. (This may be why we expect the wicked mother in "Hansel and Gretel" to be a step-mother rather than the natural mother of the Grimms' version of the tale.)

The story with this plot that I remember best from my child-hood is "Mother Holle." Here a widow favors her own ugly, idle daughter over a stepdaughter who is forced to do all the house-work. One day as the stepdaughter is spinning by the well, she drops her shuttle, and it falls to the bottom. Told she must go after it, she jumps into the well and loses consciousness. When she awakens she finds herself in a lovely, flower-studded meadow through which she begins to walk. She passes an oven full of bread that calls out, "O, take me out before I burn," and of course she does it. She passes an apple tree that calls, "O, shake me; I am so heavy," and, of course, she does. Finally she comes to Mother Holle's little house and agrees to enter her service, to do all the housework diligently and especially to shake out her featherbed vigorously—for when the feathers fly, there is snow on earth. Though she is so much better off with this old woman than at home, after a time she gets homesick and asks if she can go back to her own family. Mother Holle agrees and takes her to the door that leads back to the other world. As the girl passes under the gate a heavy shower of gold rains upon her. The gold sticks to her so that she is covered with it as she returns to her mother and sister. The mother, of course, is eager to obtain the same good fortune for her own daughter, whom she tells to go to the well, drop her shuttle, and jump in after it. But when this daughter walks through the lovely meadow, she refuses to respond to the cry of the baking bread or the burdened apple tree. She agrees to apprentice herself to Mother Holle and works well enough on the first day, but on each subsequent day she does less work more sulkily, and soon the old woman asks her to leave. Expectantly, the lazy girl stands under the open doorway, but instead of gold a bucketful of pitch is emptied over her.

I remember this story well, including the clear sense that I knew exactly which daughter I was and was pretty sure that my mother knew, too. I didn't know then that Mother Holle is an ancient Germanic underworld goddess[11] and, of course, could have had no intimation of how the first girl's meeting with Mother Holle echoes Psyche's meeting with Persephone, nor of how the envious relationship between the girls parallels that between Psyche and her sisters. Uncovering these connections now helps me see how right the Grimms were in their conviction that the folktales they had collected connect us to an age-old wisdom.

In the story "The Hut in the Forest," three daughters are each in turn sent into the forest to take their woodcutter father his supper. Each loses her way and stops for the night in a hut where an old man lives with a hen, a cock, and a cow as his only companions. The older two make supper for the old man and themselves, but give no thought to the animals. After they fall asleep, he locks them up in his cellar. When the turn of the youngest comes, she spontaneously feeds the animals before preparing her own supper and thereby not only saves herself but breaks the spell long ago cast on the old man, who is really a handsome young prince. The two are married—and the older sisters are sentenced to be servants until they grow kinder and have learned to show love not only toward humankind but toward animals as well.

In "The Three Little Birds" the two older sisters are jealous of the third sister not only because she is married to the king and they only to his chief ministers, but because they are sterile and she is about to have a child. As soon as the child is born, they seize it from her and drown it and then tell the king his wife has given birth to a dog. The same thing happens after the birth of a second son and after the birth of a daughter, except that on the third occasion the king is told his wife has borne a cat. This is too much for him; he is finally persuaded that his queen is a witch and orders her imprisoned. Meanwhile the three drowned children have been rescued by a fisherman who raises them in his own family. When they grow up the second son meets up with the king while both are hunting in the woods. They piece together the true story; the wife is released from prison, and her two false sisters are burnt.

The most familiar of these stories is undoubtedly "Cinderella." That this tale, which Bruno Bettelheim sees as by far the most powerful of all fairy-tale renditions of sibling jealousy, should be a tale of jealousy between sisters seems an apt acknowledgment of the intensity of female-female relationships. The ending in the Grimms' version (different from the Walt Disney version more familiar to many Americans) makes clear that such jealousy is sometimes beyond forgiveness. After Cinderella has married the prince, her two stepsisters naturally try to curry her favor. But, as the Grimms tell it, to no avail: two birds fly down and pluck out their eyes; they are punished with blindness for the rest of their days.

The alternative to this popular reversal plot is the plot of essential identity, of completely harmonious complementation, represented by the story "Snow White and Rose Red." Once upon a time there was a widow with two daughters who were utterly devoted to one another and almost exactly alike, although Snow White was a little more quiet and preferred to stay in the house while Rose Red loved to run about in the meadows. One winter night a half-frozen bear knocked on the door, and the mother allowed him to sleep by the fire. He returned each night, and the girls came to love teasing and roughhousing with their clumsy guest. When spring came they reluctantly let him leave. That summer the girls, who went everywhere together, had a series of encounters with a rather nasty dwarf who was always getting himself into situations from which they helped rescue him. Instead of being grateful, he scolded them for having in the process cut off part of his prized white beard. One day they find him sorting through a bagful of precious stones. Furious at being discovered with this treasure, he curses them viciously. Just then there is a loud growl and the bear reappears. The dwarf pleads, "Spare me; take these two wicked girls, they'd be tender morsels for you." But instead the bear attacks the dwarf, joyfully greets the girls, and is immediately transformed into a handsome prince. For a moment we think, now they'll have to differentiate, there's only one prince!—but out of nowhere his brother appears and so Snow White marries their old playmate and Rose Red weds the brother.

In his discussion of "Cinderella" Bettelheim wonders whether the selfish stepsisters may have been deprived by having only an indulgent mother.[12] Von Franz, in her analysis of this story, asks if Snow White and Rose Red may have been prevented from differentiating by knowing only an all-loving mother.[13] Mothers seem obviously to play a prominent role in both plots; they make separation very difficult for their daughters, who then play out the drama of disengagement vis-à-vis one another. Rivalry is lived out on the plane of envy, not action, or is entirely repressed. These tales present no models of sisterly differentiation that issue in harmonious relationship—only either undying emnity or symbiosis. We feel the *intensity* of these sister-sister relationships—"I can only be me if you don't exist or if you are just like me"—we sense how exaggerated it is, and how true. This intensity, this struggle to affirm our separate existence, is what seems most different when we compare sisterly to brotherly experience.

Despite their simple, repetitive plots and characters these stories do help us see some important aspects of sibling relationships—as these relationships are experienced in childhood and as they stay alive in us still. For many of us it is very likely such tales that first initiated us into archetypal experience, into the recognition of the connections between our own lives and ancient recurrent patterns of action and feeling, character and situation.

Nevertheless the stories do not satisfy our longing for a more mature understanding of sibling experience, an understanding incorporating a more complex morality, a more subtle sense of our inner life. To see siblings as simply opposites *or* identical, as helpers *or* rivals, does not do justice to our adult perspectives, though it may correspond to momentary responses in childhood. (I suspect that even then these views are not reified; the same sister who one day is experienced as the most different person in the whole world on the next day seems to be just like me in almost every way. Yesterday we were enemies; today allies.)

There is so much to sibling experience—that as an adult I want given imaginal expression—that the fairy-tale genre cannot provide. Fairy-tales give us no sense of how the relationship might look from the other's perspective. How would Cinderella's stepsisters tell the story? Because these stories focus on only the phase of the relationship that marks the transition out of childhood, they provide no illumination of the meaning of adult interactions among siblings. Their concern is with the role of siblings in the process of ego formation, not with how siblings might retard or further our later attempts to transcend ego-identification. Fairy tales do not communicate the overwhelming importance of the subtle, ambiguous differences that distinguish one sibling from another. Nor do we receive from them a sense of the idiosyncratic and unique features of sibling experience, of the great variety of sisterly and brotherly ways of being. Their focus is on plots of reconciliation and just retribution. By definition, in this genre there is no real appreciation of the profound significance of human experiences of tragedy and death.

Fairy tales seem naturally to lead us to the more mature view of sibling experience available in mythology, where we must deal with conflicting sets of stories and the conflict between moral perspectives. The longing for a deeper insight than fairy tales can give us led me to look to the testimony of the Greek myths.

3. Psyche and Her Sisters

On the way from fairy tale to myth I want, however, to pause to reflect on an intermediate story, Apuleius' "Cupid and Psyche," from which this book takes its title. This late classical tale, often referred to as "Amor and Psyche" or "Eros and Psyche," has intrigued depth psychologists from Freud to Bettelheim, from Jung to Hillman. Most of those who have responded to the tale have been men; their readings have focused on the tension between Aphrodite and Psyche or on the reunion between Psyche and Eros.[1] They have largely ignored the dimension of the story that as a female reader I have found most intriguing: its rendering of the relationship between Psyche and her sisters.

You probably remember the story, which begins: "Once upon a time there lived a king and queen who had three very beautiful daughters . . . " The third of these sisters, Psyche, was so beautiful that she was worshiped as an incarnation of Aphrodite. Even after her two sisters were married to kings, no mortal dared court her. When her perplexed father consulted the Delphic oracle, he was told to abandon his daughter on a lonely mountaintop where she would be wed to a deadly monster. Meanwhile Aphrodite, ignored and jealous, had told her son Eros to look for the maiden and punish her by making her fall in love with some ignoble wretch. When Eros finds Psyche, he is so taken by the beauty of the abandoned maiden that he falls in love with her himself and has her brought to his magnificent palace. Each night in the dark he comes to make love to her but warns her that she may not know who he is.

On one of his nightly visits Eros tells Psyche that her sisters, fearing her dead, are looking everywhere for some trace of her. Warning her that it would be dangerous, he forbids her to get in touch with them. But Psyche's tears and endearments persuade him to let them be brought to the palace after all. Though overjoyed to find her safe and impressed by the splendor of her palace, they are, of course, curious about the mysterious husband. Psyche diverts their questions with lies about his youthful beauty and sends them home, but her answers only fuel their discontent with their own marriages and their envy of hers. When on a second visit she describes her spouse quite differently than at first, they begin to suspect not only that she has never seen his face but that he may be a god. This further aggravation of their envy inspires the plot against her happiness that they put into motion during their third visit.

Feigning tears, they tell Psyche that they have learned that Apollo's oracle was fulfilled after all, that her husband, apparently so loving, is in reality a dreadful monster determined to devour both her and the child she already carries in her womb. They succeed in playing on Psyche's own uneasiness at never having seen her husband and at knowing nothing of where he goes during the day. She tells them how terrifying she finds his warnings against them and his threats that should she allow herself to be persuaded to try to look upon his face her unborn child will be a mortal daughter rather than a divine son. She asks them for help. Claiming to be speaking out of sisterly devotion, they unfold their plan. She is to prepare a lantern and a razor-sharp knife so that after her love-satisfied husband has fallen asleep, she can kill the loathsome beast.

That night, intending to carry out the plan, she lights the lamp and finds that her lover is not the monster depicted by her sisters but rather a beautiful young god. In her amazed awe, she jostles the lantern. A drop of oil falls on Eros' shoulder; he awakens—and flies away as he had warned her he would.

The tale goes on, as we shall see, to recount the labors Psyche must undertake at Aphrodite's command in order to regain her lover, the last of which requires that she visit the underworld and bring Persephone's beauty box back to Aphrodite. In the end Psyche and Eros are reunited and married on Olympus, Psyche is made immortal, and she gives birth to a daughter, Pleasure.

Though perhaps partly based on older traditions and obviously a variant of the familiar "Beauty and the Beast" motif, there are no known literary antecedents to the version of this tale included by the second-century Latin poet Apuleius in his *Metamorphoses* (also known as *The Golden Ass.*) Neither myth nor fairy tale but a consciously invented allegory created to serve as a harmonic overtone to the main plot's account of Lucius' initiation into the Greco-Roman mystery cult devoted to Isis, this narrative is almost irresistibly available to psychological interpretation.

For well-educated Europeans of Freud's and Jung's time the word *psyche* immediately conjured up this story, the only classical tale in which Psyche appears. They found deeply moving its implication that *the* true story about Psyche is one that involves Eros, that the soul realizes itself in relationship, that human love is directed toward soul-making.

The story has been taken, particularly by Jungian commentators, as representing "the psychic development of the feminine." The phrasing leaves ambiguous whether what is meant is the process whereby a man integrates the so-called feminine aspects of his unconscious (the anima) or the female process of individuation. As Marie Louise von Franz has shown[2] there is much to support the notion that the story is really about *male* experience, especially when one understands the tale in terms of its role within the larger context of the novel. The story was written by the male poet Apuleius to complement his account of his male protagonist's initiation into the Isis cult. Von Franz sees Apuleius as closely identified with his hero's struggle to free himself from a positive mother complex. She is especially alert to the way the ending of the inset tale, Psyche's returning to a passive femininity, her becoming again someone who needs to be rescued by a male, plays into male fantasies about femininity. The transposition of the couple to Olympus, their removal from the world of human struggle, similarly seems to her to suggest an unresolved anima fantasy. She sees the birth of Psyche's daughter as a symbol of repetition, of the reappearance of the anima problem. Von Franz helps us understand why most of the interpreters have been men and why women have been less appreciative of a tale that implies that a woman's wholeness is constellated only in a heterosexual relation and that the culmination of the female individuation journey consists in giving up and being rescued by a male.

Yet von Franz's interpretation seems at places just as forced as the more usual one. To read the story as only about the male and his anima seems to wrench it out of its own shape. As she herself notes, although Apuleius may have consciously constructed the tale, it contains more than he knowingly put into it, including echoes of the female experience that helped shape the Eleusinian and Isis mysteries. That "more" is part of what gives the tale its ongoing life and its power to speak to women as well as men. Within the novel the tale is told by a woman to a woman, by an old drunken woman who keeps house for a group of bandits to the young bride, Charite, whom those bandits have abducted. (Lucius had persuaded his mistress to anoint him with a magical ointment he had hoped would transform him into a god and instead found himself transformed into an ass. The bandits bring the ass home and thus Lucius—and we—get to overhear the old woman's tale.) Though the crone gives her story about Psyche's abduction a reassuringly "happy" ending, Charite's own story will end less happily, with her husband's death and her own suicide. Perhaps the old woman knew all along that the ending is not really the point.

Like other women discontent with the Psyche story as relayed to me, I had found another story, the myth of Persephone and Demeter, more true to my own experiences of love and confusion, transformation and reunion, more relevant to the search for Her initiated by my dream of the underground cave. I owe much to my engagement with the dread underworld goddess, yet also acknowledge that there are aspects of the myth associated with her that, if taken as paradigmatic of female individuation, are just as problematical as those that I question in the Psyche story. I think, for instance, of the myth's presentation of mother-child fusion as a nostalgic ideal only reluctantly abandoned and of its showing Persephone coming to her in-her-selfness only through abduction by a male. Other Greek goddesses represent alternative paradigms—but they are still *goddesses,* and that in itself has become an issue.

The discovery of the importance of sisterhood has led me to a new appreciation of Apuleius' tale. How we understand it may depend on what we focus on: Psyche's relation to Aphrodite, to Eros, or to her sisters. The sisterly relation has come into prominence for me as what most distinguishes Psyche's tale from

Persephone's—that and Psyche's humanity, her mortality. Erich Neumann, recognizing how important it is that Psyche is a mortal, says Psyche marks the ending of the mythical age: "In this tale the focus is on the *human* struggle for love and consciousness."[3] The story suggests that Psyche, female selfness, is constellated through engagement not with goddess or god but with other mortal women like herself. It is her sisters who encourage her to become conscious—though they may do so out of envy and with seductive guile. The end of the story disappoints because Psyche is no longer human. Von Franz is right, that part needs to be rewritten, or perhaps just omitted. We don't need the deus ex machina resolution, don't need a happy ending, anywhere near as much as we need a true story.

Before Apuleius personified Psyche the word was used by the Greeks to refer to the human soul, a life-giving principle not concerned with physical movement or ordinary consciousness. Because associated with life, breath, air, the psyche was sometimes imagined in later poetry as a butterfly, fragile, insubstantial, and beautiful. The *psyche* was associated with sexual generativity and with the inspiration available in moments of ecstasy and madness. It is the aspect of the human being, male or female, that dreams and that persists after death, that lives in Hades. Though without physical substance, it preserves the unique form of the individual; it is shadow, image—inhabiting the two realms of image that according to Homer lie side by side, the world of dream and the underworld. In Plato *psyche* has come to refer to the immortal aspect of our being, our capacity for knowing the real and enduring, our consciousness—an intuitive, imaginal consciousness attuned to non-empirical reality, attentive to that which immersion in ordinary waking life concerns tends to make us forget. In the *Phaedo* Socrates expresses his confidence that his *psyche* will persist after he ceases to breathe and his conviction that true *psyche therapeia*, attendance to soul, consists in preparation for death.[4]

Even in Apuleius' tale Psyche is connected to Hades: her last, most important task, the one she must undertake on her own, is to enter the underworld and there receive from Persephone a beauty box. I take this to be a beauty available only from the goddess of death, a beauty that comes from our knowledge of death, of our mortality. It was this aspect of the tale that most moved Freud.[5] He considers the story in the same essay in which he discusses the fairy tales "The Six Swans" and the "Seven Ravens" and also Shakespeare's *The Merchant of Venice* and *King Lear*. Freud is fascinated with the recurrent appearance in mythology and literature of a situation in which a hero must make a choice among three sisters. He believes that the sisters are in some sense always the Fates, and that the third, chosen sister, is in some sense always the goddess of death. That she should be perceived as the most beautiful recalls, he suggests, the ancient identity between the goddess of love and the goddess of death. Freud introduces "wish-fulfillment" as explanation for the reversal whereby the inevitable becomes the chosen and what is chosen is no longer a figure of terror but the fairest and most desirable of women. Yet this lovely woman retains certain uncanny characteristics, certain traits that betray her relation to death. Freud reminds us of how Psyche's wedding is celebrated like a funeral, how her third task requires her to descend into the underworld and how afterward she sinks into a deathlike sleep. To choose Psyche is to allow the third sister to take us into her arms; it entails coming to terms with the inevitability of our own death. Freud, of course, is emphasizing the *male's* choice of the third sister. When men are still caught in the hero's resistence to death it will come like Thanatos, aggressively seizing the unprepared; but for those reconciled to "the silent goddess of death," she comes like Persephone to the ancient Oedipus, "opening in love the unlit door of earth." The association of womb and tomb, of femininity and death, has an especial significance in the psychology of men. Yet it may also be true for women that truly to know Psyche is to see her in her sisterly context—and thereby to come to an acceptance of our own finitude.

Most Jungian interpreters have failed to emphasize the centrality of the relationship between Psyche and her sisters—and have paid more attention to her apotheosis than to that deathlike sleep. They have viewed the tale as an allegory about a male's integration of his femininity, his anima, or about the female journey from unconscious to conscious relatedness. Their focus falls on the tension between Aphrodite and Psyche, (understood as the conflict between the arhetypal mother that discourages consciousness and the anima that encourages individuation) or on the relation between Psyche and Eros.

Robert Johnson may give us a clue as to the meaning of this evasion: "I am personally terrified of the sister quality in a woman," he observes, as he comes to that part of the tale in which the jealous sisters make their appearance.[6] Neumann, too, speaks of the sisters as representing "the man-hating matriarchate" and sees them as having the unfortunate power to evoke a regressive feminine attitude in Psyche.

Somehow the sisters and Aphrodite represent an aspect of feminine energy that is terrifying to men—but that women may respond to differently. After all, as Bachofen saw clearly,[7] Aphrodite is *not* an advocate of undifferentiated consciousness in this tale; she is instead the one who imposes the tasks that force Psyche to discover herself. The fears about merging that Neumann (and even Hillman) associate with Aphrodite are foreign to the tale—but not to male psychology. Women, too, need to separate from mothers but not as radically, not as forcibly, as men, and so fusion may not pose quite so terrifying a threat to us.

The tale also makes clear that it is not necessarily men (or the animus) who support the female quest. Aphrodite and Psyche's sisters both push her toward consciousness; Eros would happily have kept her in the dark. The sisters are not the seductively beautiful anima figures a man might long for as psychopomp (guide to the innerworld)—but they are *Psyche's* sisters, precisely the sisters able to push her in the way her soul requires. I find it profoundly significant that *the* story about Psyche is a story in which it is the interactions among sisters that constellate psyche and teach what a reciprocal rather than a symbiotic loving might be.

James Hillman has some sense of this dimension of the tale. He understands it to be not about the male *or* the female search for self but rather about the human search for soul-making relationship.[8] He sees "Amor and Psyche" as helping us move beyond myths that focus on parent-child involvement and that keep us entangled with early childhood issues toward a perspective that celebrates the connection between siblings in which libido flows into the mutuality of soul-making. But by focusing on contra-sexual sibling experience, by seeing the relation between Eros and Psyche as like a brother-sister relationship, Hillman misses the interaction between sisters that actually occurs in the tale.

Only C. S. Lewis in his novel *Till We Have Faces* focuses on Psyche's relation to her sisters.[9] He gives us the fully rounded characterizations of the sisters that are missing in the original. He retells the tale from the perspective of one of the sisters who believes that all her interventions in Psyche's life, including the suggestion that she discover the true identity of her darkly hidden bridegroom, have been motivated by love. In Apuleius' version, after Eros has left her, Psyche seeks out each sister and tells her that Eros, angry at Psyche's betrayal, has announced that he will marry the sister instead. Each then proceeds to the mountaintop from which Eros had abducted Psyche and there falls to her death. Lewis has the sisters live on. Toward the end of her life the oldest discovers to her horror that all her love has really been motivated by her jealousy, that the physical ugliness that she has always acknowledged is matched by an ugliness of soul. Yet the coming to terms with the shadow side of her love becomes the medium of a difficult soul-making, and at the end she learns: "You, too, are Psyche." Lewis's retelling gives us a heroine whose entire struggle is lived out on the human plane and helps us see how, in the original version as well, it is sisters who serve as the mediums of revelation.

The sisters serve as shadow and as helpers. Their ambivalence toward Psyche seems typical: they mourn when they believe she has died, rejoice to discover she is still alive, envy her apparent good fortune, and inadvertently provide her with the provocation she most requires. Despite Psyche's happiness with her gentle though mysterious lover, she misses her sisters and refuses to comply with Eros' demand that she break off with them. When the sisters come to visit her, they challenge Psyche's romantic account of her marriage relationship. They may speak out of envy—they are less beautiful, their marriages less idyllic, their palaces less grand—but their words serve to start her on her journey out of naive self-satisfaction toward a more conscious, more individual loving.

Reading Apuleius' tale, we may feel that Psyche is too naive and too easily overwhelmed by suicidal despair when her over-positive view of things is challenged. Her sisters, on the other hand, are too skeptical, too tied to outer world reality. Like Demeter they articulate an upper-world perspective. But whereas in the Homeric Hymn Persephone's story is told from Demeter's perspective, in Apuleius the story is told, not from the outlook of the sisters but from Psyche's—or, as von Franz would insist, from the masculine perspective of Eros or Lucius or Apuleius.

In any case, Psyche's relation to Eros is given a value denied Persephone's relation to Hades, and the many parallels between the tales are obscured. For instance, though his seizing of Psyche is interpreted as rescue, Eros is initially just as much an abductor as Hades. Like Hades he transports his prize into an unconscious realm—though in Psyche's story the benign, beautiful fantasy aspect of this beyond-reality realm is emphasized. Von Franz sees that as the *problem*—this Eros is not really worthy of Psyche's love, is really but a *puer aeternus,* not the cosmogonic Eros of the Orphics or the mighty *daimon* of Plato. Apuleius' tale centers on Psyche's search to be reunited with Eros as the Homeric Hymn centers on Demeter's search for her daughter while deemphasizing the daughter's reunion with her under-world spouse. Yet Persephone is as bound to Hades by the pomegranate seed she has swallowed as Psyche is to Eros by his seed growing within her.

The "Amor and Psyche" tale was written and has been interpreted so as to communicate that the sisters are wrong and evil—that they are unambivalently envious, spiteful, cruel, that they represent a regressive, man-hating matriarchal phase, that of course the abducting god, the heterosexual marriage, represent Psyche's true fulfillment. Yet Neumann does acknowledge that, despite its negative form, the sisters' antimasculine, murderous agitation embodies the beginnings of a higher feminine consciousness that determines Psyche's whole subsequent development. "Something in her which may be designated negatively as matriarchal aggression or positively as a tendency toward consciousness . . . drove her imperiously to emerge from the darkness."[10]

After Eros has left her, Psyche is overwhelmed by the tasks Aphrodite imposes. Confronted with the huge pile of grains she must sort, Psyche despairs until a whole colony of ants appears and quickly does the impossible task for her. Freud tells us that in dreams or other imaginal structures small animals like bees and ants represent siblings in their helpful aspect. I believe that here, too, the ants are sisterly figures come to help with the process of sorting through. (Indeed, a deep understanding of the meaning of sisterhood would lead us to recognize such creatures of the natural world as our relatives and would not allow us to interpret them simply as Psyche's "natural instincts.")

(The helpers with Psyche's second and third tasks are admittedly more difficult to work into the sister motif. I do believe, though, that the reed can be associated to the Isis-Osiris mysteries, to the marsh of reeds where the Egyptians thought life begins, to the reeds growing from Osiris' mummified body that express the Egyptian hope for life's renewal after death—a renewal that Isis' sisterly devotion makes possible. And I like to imagine that the eagle who helps Psyche with her third task is the same eagle that was sent by Zeus to carry off Ganymede, representing not the Zeus of patriarchy but the Zeus sensitive to the pull of same-sex love.)

Psyche's last task requires that she go to Hades to secure Persephone's beauty box. Here for the first time Psyche must proceed without help from any animal. Here in this confrontation with mortality, nothing and no one can substitute for her. To enter Hades in a way that will allow her to leave after obtaining the ointment, Psyche must refuse help or even pity to an overburdened donkey driver, a floating corpse, and a bent old weaving woman. In the Grimms' fairy tale "Mother Holle," salvation comes to the sister who helps in similar circumstances and perdition to the sister who refuses, but Psyche must take on the sister's shadow energy herself. She brings the box safely out of Hades and then cannot resist looking inside.

The continuation of the story beyond Psyche's opening of the box rings as false to me as it does to von Franz. The given ending (with Psyche made an immortal resident of Olympus) returns Psyche to the unreal situation of the beginning where she is exalted above all mortal women. (The one part of the ending that does feel right is that Psyche's child should be a daughter rather than a son. Read as a woman's tale, that is gain not loss.) Because I tend to suspect a female's fantasy happy ending almost as much as a male's, I am not tempted to create a definitive alternative right ending. I prefer to see Psyche's story as one whose ending we cannot yet know but are drawn to explore, to reimagine.

As I return in imagination to the moment when Psyche has opened the beauty box and fallen into her deathlike sleep, I am left with the sense that there is something still to happen between Persephone and Psyche. I agree that it is inevitable, part of the real story, that she will do the forbidden and open the box as she had done the forbidden and lit the lantern to look at Eros' face. Surely Hillman is right: the beauty box is not to be read only as signifying a male misconception of how women are obsessed with physical beauty (as Von Franz is right that the concern with vanity would not appear at such a crucial moment in a woman's soul journey). Nor do I find satisfying Neumann's interpretation of the beauty box as representing the danger of narcissim, of unrelatedness. The beauty to which Persephone but not Aphrodite has access is the beauty that comes with an intimate, inner knowledge of death—the ultimate beauty of the psyche. I imagine a Psyche who, putting on this beauty ointment, discovers that the real aim of her journey all along has been not the reunion with Eros, not her own divinization, but the meeting with Persephone and the discovery that *they* are sisters, sister doubles, one immortal, one mortal. I think of Rilke's Eurydice, for whom the reunion with Orpheus had lost its savor:

> She was deep within herself, like a woman heavy
> with child, and did not see the man in front
> or the path ascending steeply into life.
> Deep within herself. Being dead
> filled her beyond fulfillment.[11]

I imagine a Psyche no longer bound to Eros.

Yet though Persephone may be Psyche's sister, Psyche, the mortal human woman, is mine. From her I have begun to understand that to know what it is to be a human female self comes through knowing deeply what it is to be sistered and to sister. This story in no way sentimentalizes sisterhood. Psyche's sisters were envious and cruel—and yet provided the instigation necessary to her journey toward self, toward *psyche*. They reappear as the helpful ants and as the dread goddess. My rereading, added to the many that have preceded it, is intended to substantiate the proposal with which I introduced this book: the story of Psyche and her sisters serves as an initiation into the mysteries of sisterhood, opens us to an appreciation of how our sisterly relationships challenge and sustain us—at the same time that we inevitably also fail and betray one another.

Yet the tale is only a gateway; essentially an allegory, it lacks the full richness of character, plot, and morality found in true myth. It affirms the centrality of sisterly experience in female life without really doing justice to its complexity. For that we must turn to older myths.

4. Mythic Siblings

The turn to mythology is for me in the first instance almost inevitably a return to Greek mythology. In part, no doubt, this is because these are the myths that I know have shaped my understanding of and my emotional response to sibling experience. But it is also because, as George Steiner observes, the handful of stories told and retold by the Greek epic and tragic poets have come to constitute an essential code of reference for the Western imagination.[1] Because until now so much of our literature and our institutions has been shaped by these origins, our own assumptions, our very feelings, have also inevitably been influenced by them. Obviously, this is less true for those not educated in the dominant culture, as it also obviously raises problems for women because of the heavily misogynist cast of much of this culture-shaping literature. Nevertheless, I am persuaded we cannot afford to ignore these traditions.

Freud, too, was persuaded of the imaginative-formal decisiveness of this particular mythology for the Western psyche—a conviction that Jung, with his emphasis on archetype rather than myth, did not share. The difference between archetype and myth is an important one: archetypes are ideal universal forms, generalizations; myths are stories. The archetypal sister and brother are abstractions; mythological sisters or brothers are defined by their relationships and situations. In myth a woman is not a sister in herself, in her essence, but in relation to this sister or that brother, in a particular context, a particular family history, a particular crisis. Myths give us a sense of the great variety of ways in which one may be a sister or brother. Many of these ways feel eerily familiar and in that looser sense are archetypal: these particular modes of sibling interaction still recur both outwardly and in a more inner sense. I also feel strongly these mythic prototypes do not exhaust the shapes sibling experience may take or what it may mean. Not only are the myths of other cultures also relevant, but we need to go on, to reimagine sisterhood in new ways. Yet I believe it is an illusion to think we can do it from scratch, and would be suspicious of completely idealized versions, not rooted in our own and our culture's experience.

As I noted earlier, when I first became intrigued with trying to understand what it meant to be and have a sister, I had hoped that I might find a Greek goddess who would model this primary relationship for me, found there were none—but then found sisterhood to be a central theme among the mortal women of Greek mythology, the heroines of cult, epic, and tragedy.

There are in Greek mythology also groups of sisters at an intermediate level between that occupied by the major divinities and that inhabited by us humans: the Horae, the Graces, the Gorgons, the Furies, and the Fates. But because the individual figures within these groups are barely distinguishable from one another, and there is little dramatic in their mutual interactions, there seems nothing relevant to our experience in their representation of sisterhood.

There is also an amazing tale of a family of fifty sisters, the Danaids, whose father's twin brother had fifty sons. The maidens are forcibly betrothed to their cousins, but the father gives each a dagger and orders her to kill her husband in the bridal chamber—which all but one, Hypermnestra (an ancestress of Klytemnestra), do. In punishment of this heinous crime they are sent to Hades, where everlastingly they try to fill leaky jars with water. In Aeschylus' *The Suppliant Maidens* these daughters appear as the chorus, speaking with one voice. (According to Aristotle, Greek tragedy begins with this communal "I.") But though we may sympathize with the maidens' plight, their story does little to help us sort through the "I" and "you" of human sisterly bonds.

However, when we turn to the later tragedies we discover powerful female figures who become themselves through their struggles with one another. Among these heroines sisterly bonds are highly significant. The sisterhood of Helen and Klytemnestra, Iphigenia and Elektra, Ariadne and Phaedra, Procne and Philomela, Antigone and Ismene, is essential to who they are. One cannot adequately tell their stories without including it. They themselves each view their character and fate as inextricably intertwined with that of their sister. The stories that are retold in Greek myth, epic, and drama communicate a more profound, complex, and humanly relevant understanding of sisterhood than I have found anywhere else. These representations make evident the polymorphous and multidimensional reality of the bond; they show its pervasive influence; they reveal how it is experienced from both sides.

As I have looked at the Greek myths about siblings I have found myself focusing much more on the literary versions than I did in my book on the goddesses, where I tried to get behind the work of the male poets of patriarchal classical Athens to earlier preliterary matrifocal strata of the tradition and to evidences of women's cultic relation to the divinities. But although some of the heroes and heroines may have been gods or goddesses before the establishment of the Olympian pantheon and though some were still part of a vital cult of the dead long after Homer, I found much less extraliterary evidence concerning these figures than for the goddesses.

My decision is also positively motivated. I have found myself deeply moved by the understandings of these characters communicated by the tragedians and knew I wanted to consider, to absorb, to reflect on their particular representations. The three major tragedians—Aeschylus, Sophokles, and Euripides—have each, for example, articulated their own version of Elektra. The essential shape of her story was a given; they do not disagree about her deeds. But the differences in their characterizations of her motivation and her morality, have led me toward a fuller appreciation of the complexities inherent in her myth.

The dramatic poets retell the myths associated with the heroic age, with the lives of human not divine characters. The tragedies focus on moments of crisis and lysis, change and revelation. Tragedy arises out of the human necessity of making decisions, out of the experience of trying to reconcile impossibly contradictory claims, out of the discovery that the gods are not to be trusted because they represent competing values, out of the bitter wisdom that our own natural faults and ignorance seem to issue in overwhelming, unremitting consequences. Because the heroes and heroines struggle with the same moral ambiguities and complexities that perplex us, we sense the possibility of a different kind of relationship to them than to the gods and goddesses. Perhaps what makes me want to linger over the tragedians' representations of mortal characters is the more intimate access they have to these fellow humans than they do to divine beings.

I am also struck by the degree to which Greek tragedy is about the transition from matrifocal to patrifocal culture, and about the complex losses and gains associated with that change. The perspective is male: the transition to a more impersonal, abstract conception of justice is validated as the necessary resolution to the unending cycles of blood vengeance associated with a social system based entirely on kinship bonds—and shown as still precarious. In the world of tragedy the power of the mother is still so fearsome that her very role in human conception must be denied, as it is in Athene's famous speech in *The Eumenides*. These dramas abound in portraits of powerful women. Though in terms of cult centers the heroes may have outnumbered the heroines six to one;[2] in drama almost the reverse seems to obtain! The women that occupy center stage, from Aeschylus' Klytemnestra to Euripides' Medea, embody female strength as thwarted and distorted by male power, and therefore, as become even more threatening to men. The poets are men, their perspective is male, and yet their dramas enable *us* to glimpse a different way of telling the same stories—a way that communicates a female perspective—a way foretold by the chorus of women in *Medea*

> Legends now shall change direction, Women's life have
>   glory.
> Honor comes to the female sex.
> Woman shall be a theme of slanderous tales no more.
>
> The songs of poets from bygone times shall cease
> to harp on our faithlessness.
> It was not to our minds that Phoebus, lord of melody,
> granted the power to draw heavenly song from the
>   lyre:
> for if so, we would have chanted our own hymns of
>   praise
> to answer the race of man.
>
> Time in its long passage has much to tell
> of our destiny as of theirs.[3]

Although I feel the limitations of the tragedians' male perspective and know I need to go beyond it, I also know I need to start there. I need to feel my way into these persuasively rendered explorations of brotherly and sisterly experience—to try to see what in my own experience and my own spontaneous feelings is consonant with these visions and where I feel they miss or distort. Only by attending to these representations do I see clearly what I want to question, to add, to reach toward.

I am interested not only in reflections on the dramatists' powerful renditions of sister-sister interactions but also in their visions of how being sister to a sister differs from being sister to a brother, and of how the relationship between brothers differs from that between sisters. I know their understanding of gender to be more complex than in the fairy-tale tradition we examined earlier. I am curious about how these visions correspond to my own experience, curious about how and why sisterhood and brotherhood differ—then and now.

In this chapter I will look at the Greek mythic traditions about brother-brother and sister-brother relations. The consideration of this mythology's representation of the sister-sister relationship is so central to my whole exploration that it clearly deserves a chapter of its own. Although many of us have known these tales since we were children, although they may reverberate within our psyches now more compellingly than we know—it is nonetheless important to tell them again, to attend consciously to these representations of sibling experience.

To the Greeks brotherhood was clearly the more visible relationship. Even among the Olympians, brotherhood is more honored than sisterhood—seen as more central and less problematic. For the male divinities having Zeus' fatherhood in common seems sufficient to create the fraternal tie; they need not also share a mother. (Indeed, that Ares and Hephaistos are both sons of Hera as well as Zeus seems to be precisely what underlies the unmitigated antagonism between them. Their relationship suggests that just as it is mothers who spur heroes on to undertake one impossible task after another, so it is mothers who inspire and secretly delight in rivalry between their sons.) Often the fraternal relationships between immortals are depicted as beautifully tender. Among the most delightful of all

Greek mythological tales is the account in *The Homeric Hymn to Hermes* of the affectionate teasing and trickery that passes between the newborn Hermes and his elder brother Apollo; among the most moving of all Greek statues is the one at Olympia of the now grown Hermes holding to his shoulder the infant Dionysos.

Indeed, so revered is the bond between brothers that it is recognized in cult, in the homage paid to the Dioscuri, the twins, Kastor and Polydeukes. Both were sons of Leda (mother also to Helen and Klytemnestra); Kastor was son to her kingly spouse, Tynadareus, and thus mortal; Polydeukes was immortal because his father was Zeus. In the course of one of their many adventures together, Kastor was killed. Polydeukes, who valued his brother more than his life, persuaded Zeus to allow him to share his immortality with Kastor. Together always, they spend half their days in Hades and half on Olympus. They appear in the heavens as the constellation Gemini. As brothers, as an inseparable unit, the Dioscuri were widely worshiped throughout Greece, especially in their native Sparta.

The Dioscuri represent neither the bond between divine brothers nor that between human brothers but rather, precisely, the bond between a divine and a human brother. Essentially the same relationship exists between Herakles, the son of Zeus, and his mortal twin, Iphikles, who spends most of his time as a minor helpful companion to Herakles during some of the latter's most arduous labors. At one point though, according to tradition, Iphikles gets tired of this role and allies himself with Eurystheus, Herakles' lifelong persecutor. It isn't easy always to be the lesser figure.

The Dioscuri were worshiped by committed male friends and lovers as embodying the ideal expression of deep male-male bonding. Their representation of brotherhood as a beautifully supportive but essentially extroverted, action-oriented relationship served as a model for all close male-male bonds. Although many of the prominent heroes in Greek mythology have no actual brother, they are often accompanied on their adventures by a surrogate brother, an inseparable companion, a cousin or close friend. The bond between such male pairs is patterned after that of the Spartan twins.

The most famous such brotherlike pair are Achilles and Patroklos. As a young boy, after accidentally killing a playmate,
Patroklos went to Peleus' court for purification. He became an
attendant of Peleus' son, Achilles, and eventually his lover. The
two went to Troy together, and both withdrew from the fighting
when Achilles felt insulted by Agamemnon. But when the Trojans begin to defeat the Greeks, Patroklos persuaded Achilles
to let him return to the battle wearing Achilles' armor. Mistak-
ing him for Achilles, Hector kills Patroklos. The distraught
Achilles refuses to allow his lover to be buried until he has
taken vengeance by killing a great number of Trojans, including
Hector. Later, when Achilles himself is killed, their bones are
intermingled in one grave. (When Patroklos goes into battle
with Achilles' armor he is called Achilles' *therapon*, the one who
takes on himself the suffering of the other, a particular kind of
alter ego, one that inspires our notion of therapist.) The relationship between Achilles and Patroklos is acclaimed in Plato's
Symposium as the ideal paradigm of eros between men.

Although he undertakes his earlier adventures alone, Theseus
in later life becomes closely involved with Peirithoüs, the rash,
impious son of Ixion (the would-be seducer of Hera and first
human murderer, who ended up chained in Hades to a fiery,
ever-revolving wheel). The two engage in a series of crazy, fruitless adventures inspired by a mad vow that they will help each
other marry daughters of Zeus. First they try to abduct Helen,
who is quickly rescued by her brothers, the Dioscuri. Then they
descend to Hades with the intent of kidnapping Persephone;
there they unthinkingly sit down on the seats of forgetfulness
and find themselves stuck, unable to get up. Eventually Herakles
rescues Theseus, but Pirithoüs is left to his fate. Pirithoüs seems
to be a kind of shadow for Theseus—an exaggerated version of
his own younger self. The middle-aged hero who doesn't know
how to settle down turns to his adventure-loving friend in the
hope of escaping the tedium and responsibilities of maturity.
The Theseus-Pirithoüs relationship suggests the limitations of
the Dioscuri model—we cannot really imagine the twins as
adult men. It is not incidental to their fate that heroes die
young.

These representations of brother*like* relationship come from the epics; the tragic poets seem to have been pulled to the more complex, more tragic, interactions between actual brothers. Recalling the dramatists' version of fraternal experience will further illuminate our own. Their theme: the sacrality of the blood tie and the dreadful consequences of its seemingly fated, inescapable violation.

The family history of the Mycenaeans that so fascinated the tragedians is from the beginning a history of fraternal strife, of murder and adultery. It begins with Tantalus, a son of Zeus who resented that, though child to a god, he was mortal. In revenge he invited the gods to a feast at which he served them his own son, Pelops, cut up and cooked into a stew. Demeter ate the shoulder but the other gods, having discovered what was going on before beginning their meal, put Pelops back together again (with an ivory shoulder) and restored him to life. Tantalus they consigned to everlasting torture in Hades; eternally, he reaches for food and drink that remains forever just out of his grasp.

It is Pelops who draws down the curse that shapes his family's destiny for generations. His story begins like a fairy tale—with a royal father's announcement that he will give his daughter to that suitor able to beat him in a chariot race. Unlike a fairy-tale hero, Pelops wins by cheating, by bribing the king's charioteer, Myrtilus, to loosen the linchpin on the royal chariot. The king not only loses the race but is killed, and Pelops goes off with the daughter as his prize. The charioteer had evidently hoped to share in the prize and, feeling cheated when Pelops insists on keeping his bride for himself, tries to rape her. Pelops catches him, seizes him by the neck, and throws him into the sea—as Myrtilus flies through the air, he delivers his curse.

This curse affects the lives of Pelops' sons, Thyestes and Atreus, their sons, and the sons of their sons. Though Thyestes and Atreus join forces early on to murder their half brother, Chrysippus (whose seduction by Laios when he was a young boy brought down the curse that plagued Laios' house for three generations), they spend the rest of their lives in unremitting conflict. Their quarrel begins over the issue of which is to be the king of Mycenae. Both agree it should go to the one possessing the fleece of a golden-haired lamb—Atreus because he knows he had hidden such a fleece in a box, Thyestes because he has secretly been given this box by Atreus' wife, Aerope, with whom he is having a clandestine affair. Initially the throne goes to Thyestes, but with Zeus' aid Atreus soon takes it from him and sends Thyestes into exile. After learning of his wife's adultery, Atreus pretends to make peace with his brother and invites him back to a feast—at which he serves him a stew whose main ingredients are the cut-up pieces of Thyestes' sons. The Pelopid house will thereafter be haunted for generations by the Erinyes, the vengeance-seeking spirits, of these children. Imagine the horror, the sense of inexpungible pollution involved in learning that one has—even if unknowingly, unconsciously— eaten one's own children. Imagine the unremitting hatred one would feel toward a brother who could trick one into such a deed.

An oracle tells Thyestes that the only way he can avenge himself on his brother is to have a child by his own daughter, Pelopia. According to another version Thyestes rapes Pelopia, not recognizing her as his daughter. Soon after, Atreus, also failing to recognize her, falls in love with this same Pelopia. He marries her, brings her back to Mycenae, and raises the child conceived of her union with Thyestes (whose parentage no one knows) as his own son. When this child, Aegisthus, grows up he learns the true story of his origin, kills Atreus, and restores the throne to his natural father, Thyestes.

Now Atreus' sons by Aerope, Agamemnon and Menelaus, undertake to avenge their father's murder. They induce Tyndareus, king of Sparta and father of Klytemnestra and Helen, to help them oust Thyestes from Mycenae. Agamemnon kills Thyestes' son, Tantalus, and marries Tantalus' wife Klytemnestra—after tearing her baby from her breast and dashing out its brains. He then uses his wealth and power to win Helen for Menelaus. When Menelaus is cuckolded by Helen, Agamemnon reminds Helen's other suitors of their promise to support her husband if the marriage is ever in threat, and the Trojan war begins.

On the surface, Agamemnon and Menelaus are devoted brothers, but the Greek poets reveal them as inwardly weak and as actually despising each other. Each seems to project his own weakness onto his brother. Both are remembered primarily as cuckolded spouses, not as heroes. They obtain whatever immortality they have through their wives rather than through their own deeds. That they survive the war, that they come home, itself signifies that they are not heroes, that their deaths will be unheroic. From the Greek perspective heroic glory and homecoming, *kleos* and *nostos*, are irreconcilable.[4]

When the Greek army has been assembled at Aulis, Artemis becalms the winds and thus keeps the troops from sailing. Agamemnon is told by an oracle that only the sacrifice of his daughter, Iphigenia, will appease the goddess. Euripides shows Agamemnon, during an angry conversation with Menelaus, blaming Helen for putting him in this unbearable situation. When Menelaus responds, "You have convinced me, don't do it," Agamemnon backs off: "But I have to. The troops would never let me get away with putting familial devotion above my political responsibility." He would have preferred to blame Helen; when that does not work, he hides behind his role. Later, when Agamemnon has to confide his decision about the sacrifice to Klytemnestra and Iphigenia, he is so obsessed with his own misfortune as to be entirely unaware of the women's sorrow or fear. Agamemnon incurs guilt by acceding to his daughter's sacrifice, which will come to haunt him—yet his guilt is itself also a consequence of the guilt inherited from Atreus.

After Iphigenia's sacrifice, Agamemnon sets sail for Troy, while Klytemnestra returns to Mycenae and takes Aegisthus as her lover. The brothers fight together at Troy and share in the responsibility for the impious deeds after the Greek victory, the unnecessary killings, the rapes and abductions, the destruction of the shrines. After the war they separate, Menelaus and Helen returning to Sparta only after a long detour in Egypt, Agamemnon heading directly back toward Argos with his captive concubine, Kassandra. Upon Agamemnon's return, Aegisthus helps Klytemnestra kill Agamemnon in retribution for his own father's ouster from the throne. Later Aegisthus is in turn killed by Agamemnon's son, Orestes, who also kills his spouse-slaying mother. Menelaus has by this time returned to Sparta with the forgiven Helen. Orestes counts on his uncle's support for what he did to avenge his father's murder, but because Menelaus refuses to intercede, Orestes is found guilty of matricide and the Erinyes begin their unceasing persecution. The curse on the house finally comes to an end with Athene's acquittal of Orestes. No other family history shows so dramatically how the brotherly relation may be a cursed one, how the hatred between brothers may be passed down from one generation to the next, how it becomes something that seems to have a power of its own that the individuals involved are helpless to end.

Orestes is heir to both traditions, to that of the Dioscuri and that of the Atreides. He cannot escape the inheritance of strife but is able to bring it to resolution through his own suffering. Perhaps it helps that he is an only son, that he has no brothers (though this also means that his punishment comes directly from the Erinyes—there is no human agent available to do their work for them).

Orestes clearly wants the ideal version of brotherhood represented by his maternal uncles, the Dioscuri, to be the true one. His friendship with his cousin Pylades (whose mother was the sister of Agamemnon and Menelaus) is modeled on the twins' devotion to one another. Pylades assists Orestes in his vengeance against Klytemnestra and Aegisthus and afterward marries Orestes' sister, Elektra. Later he accompanies Orestes on the journey to Tauris, undertaken to win purification from the pollution incurred by the murders; he helps him rescue his other sister, Iphigenia, who, they learn, had been rescued from her funeral pyre at Aulis by Artemis and installed at Tauris as her priestess. The two are taken for the Dioscuri when they first arrive at Tauris and act in harmony with the attribution. When Iphigenia offers to allow Orestes to escape, he tells her he is not willing to live on at Pylades' expense. "We are brothers in everything but birth," he tells her. "Let me live through him and through his children."

Brotherly conflict also plays a central role in the history of the Theban royal house. Oedipus' own tragedy is the outworking of the curse laid on his father, Laios, for violating the code of hospitality by raping young Chrysippus while visiting Pelops' palace. Oedipus in turn just before his death curses his sons/

brothers, Eteocles and Polyneices, for having sent him into exile after his acts of patricide and incest became known. He accuses them of having violated the fraternal bond, indeed, of having forfeited their manhood. Their deeds, he says, show them to be womanly and craven, whereas his daughters have proven themselves manly and loyal. By denying Oedipus' fatherhood, they also deny their relationship to each other; by denying their brotherly relation to Oedipus, they deny the sacrality of the fraternal bond. Oedipus' curse—that they will kill one another—is in a sense but the making explicit of the curse they have already brought down upon themselves.

After sending Oedipus into exile, these brothers had initially alternated as rulers of Thebes (perhaps in echo of some ancient pattern of seasonal alternation). At one point, however, Eteocles refused to relinquish the throne when his term was up, and Polyneices decided to use foreign mercenaries to help regain it. There are no real differences of character between them—but they seem unable to stop the curse. As Eteocles cries in *Seven Against Thebes:*

> It is the God that drives this matter on.
> Since it is so—on, on with favoring wind
> this wave of hell that has engulfed for its share
> all kin of Laius . . .
>
> We are already past the care of the Gods.
> For them our death is the admirable offering.
> Why then delay, fawning upon our doom?[5]

The very lack of difference seems to require conflict as the means of differentiation—so great is the fear of fusion. Each perceives the other as enemy, as shadow. The conflict between them leads to the death of each by the other's hand. Each has to murder the other to *be*—but in doing so kills himself as well. In this incest-bound family the members are *too* closely related—and so become strangers and enemies—as in the previous generation, Laios and Oedipus, though father and son, met as strangers and enemies.

In early versions of the myth the two brothers are interchangeable, but Polyneices comes to be more prominent, whether as victim of his brother's breach of trust or as the greedy usurper willing to lead foreigners in battle against his own native city. In Aeschylus' *Seven Against Thebes* Eteocles initially seems more calm and righteous; that Polyneices carries an image of Dike, justice, on his shield, seems an obvious travesty. But as the play progresses, we discover that Eteocles is just as possessed by fury, by the Erinyes, as his brother. The curse is fulfilled; they kill each other in single combat. Mourning over the bodies of her two misguided brothers, Antigone proclaims that now they are dead, what is left is that they are brothers. The chorus confirms, "Their emnity is ended, in the earth blood-drenched their life is mingled. Very brothers are they now." Just then Creon's messenger arrives to announce that the bodies must be separated. Eteocles, for his loyalty, his blameless purity and honorable death, is to be buried in the earth he loved. His brother Polyneices, or rather Polyneices' dead body, is to be cast out unburied for the dogs to devour. Even in death he must retain his guilt. The play ends with a powerful image of the chorus dividing in two, half following one brother's corpse, half the other's. One half, challenging the civic decree, is resolved to bury Polyneices in honor of the grief common to the race voiced in Antigone's dirge over both brothers; the other half chooses to go with Eteocles "as the city and Justice jointly approve."

Despite Antigone's fervent plea, the separation of the brothers is *not* ended. The Dioscuri represent one vision of brotherhood, but Greek tragedy knows a different, deeper, darker truth.

Greek mythology also provides us with many powerful accounts of the relation between sisters and brothers. The divine prototype for this relationship is provided by Artemis and Apollo. As Walter Otto says, both are divinities "of the far"; they are self-contained, solitary, remote; enmeshment poses no threat. Both are divinities; their equality is a given. Each has her or his own sphere of power. At the human level what is given among the gods—intimacy balanced by distance, parity and mutuality, delight in similarity accompanied by enjoyment of individual difference—is never assured. It is dream, longing; it inspires hope, frustration, anger.

Again the most telling tales involved the royal families of Mycenae and of Thebes. The most horrifying tale, however, is that of Medea and the brother whom she slays, Aspyrtus. Infatuated with Jason, leader of the Argonauts, Medea uses her magical powers to help the Greeks steal the golden fleece entrusted to the care of her father, the king of Colchis. Her brother leads the Colchian pursuit of the Argonauts as they sail away with Medea and the fleece. Without compunction in choosing lover over brother, Medea helps Jason dismember the body, whose pieces they then toss into the sea one by one, thereby effectively delaying the Colchians who piously stop to gather each piece for burial.

When they return to Greece Medea attempts to secure a throne for her lover by persuading its aging occupant, Pelias, and his daughters to let her use her gifts of sorcery to restore him to youth. Following her instructions the daughters kill their father, chop his body up, and toss it into the supposedly magical caldron. Pelias fails to come back to life, and Jason temporarily becomes king. The angry citizens soon expel him, and the two move on to Corinth. Eventually Jason's ambitions lead him to decide to replace Medea with the much-younger daughter of the king of Corinth. Medea takes her revenge by murdering the intended bride—and her own two sons. The murder of Aspyrtus, the murder of Pelias, were motivated by her infatuation with Jason. When she realizes that for him power and security are all that ever really mattered, she directs against him all the daring intensity, the courage and intellect, hitherto used in his behalf. She had given up her own family for her lover and now, in sacrificing her children, does so again. She has no way of wounding him without hurting herself.

Later still, she tries to poison Theseus, the son of her second husband, Aegeus, king of Athens, in order to ensure that her own son, Medus, would inherit the throne. Caught in the attempt and banished from Athens, Medea and Medus secretly return to Colchis, where her uncle has in the meanwhile deposed and perhaps killed her father. Medea kills the usurper, and her son takes over the kingdom. "Nothing is known of Medea's death, if indeed she died at all."[6]

Medea is called a witch by those who suffer from her deeds,

but the chorus of women in Euripides' *Medea* identify with her, see her plight as akin to theirs, her courage as a source of pride. She herself is certain all along that the gods are on her side and never relents from her purpose, never repents of her deeds. At the end of the play, she escapes. She is not abandoned by the gods. Her carriage swings high out of reach, to the place reserved in Attic tragedy for the gods. Her fierce and merciless rage at oppression and betrayal made her "something more and less than human, something inhuman, a *theos*. . . . She is, at the end, a figure which personifies something permanent and powerful in the human situation."[7] The murder of her brother with which her story begins is but the first evidence of her willingness to betray even the bonds of blood for the sake of what matters still more, her autonomy.

The relationship between sisters and brothers is a central theme in the myths associated with the house of Atreus. That between Helen and her brothers, the Dioscuri, is variously represented. On the one hand, they not only rescued her from Theseus' attempted abduction when she was but a girl but also, according to Euripides, came again to the rescue of "the best and most faithful sister in the world," when she and Menelaus were imprisoned in Egypt.[8] On the other hand, one tradition about their death has it that they killed themselves in shame at her flight to Troy with Paris.

Orestes' relations to his two sisters, Iphigenia and Elektra, are each life-shaping and yet entirely distinct. There is no real overlap; he is never involved with both at the same time. In both instances he is the much younger brother, so much younger that to each he seems almost like a son.

As an infant he is brought along to Aulis by Klytemnestra and Iphigenia. When the young girl learns of her coming death, she turns to her baby brother, who cannot yet speak, and asks him to plead on her behalf. When the moment for saying her farewells arrives, she has no message for her sisters but asks Klytemnestra to nurture Orestes for her sake, as though he were *her* baby, the child she will never have.

Elektra, too, looks upon Orestes as her own son and competes with her mother for his affection. In Sophokles' *Elektra* Klytemnestra blames Elektra for having stolen Orestes from her by sending him away from Mycenae for safety after Agamemnon's murder. When Orestes returns after an eight years' absence, Elektra tells him, "Never were you your mother's love as much as mine. None was your nurse but I within that household." When she calls him, "child of the body I loved the best,"[8] we see how closely her love of Orestes is connected to her incestuously intense love of her father.

As father's daughter, Elektra wants Orestes to be his father's son—which means to continue the cycle of revenge. In Euripdes' *Orestes*, he, too, speaks of himself as a father's child: "She [Klytemnestra] was the furrow but without the father there is no child." But Orestes would have been satisfied to kill Aegisthus and to have Klytemnestra purified; it is Elektra who persuades him that both must be killed. Orestes, as Euripides represents him, is so full of betrayed love for his mother and jealousy toward her lover, that he confuses chronology and claims that Iphigenia's death occurred as punishment of his mother's adultery. He longs for a mother as faithful to her husband as Penelope to Odysseus, as nurturant of her son as Penelope of Telemachus.

Euripides' *Elektra* shows Elektra as strong, determined—and not a little mad. "I will be the one to plan my mother's death," she proclaims. Although, in her exultation after the murders are accomplished, she addresses her brother as "man of triumph sprung from our triumphant father," Orestes is much the less decisive beforehand and afterward soon inescapably reveals himself as weak and cowardly, sickened and brutalized by what they have done. Though he tries to direct his blame at Apollo, who had laid on him the duty of revenge, he says that he is now sure that his father would have urged him to let his mother live. The realization that he has killed her drives him insane. He acknowledges that maybe it wasn't Apollo who had urged the killings but a demon, maybe it was all delusion. Or maybe Apollo was wrong; certainly he seems powerless to protect Orestes now from the pursuing Furies. Maybe the blame should fall on Elektra, whom in his madness Orestes sees as one of the Furies come to attack him. In Euripides' *Orestes*, Orestes seeks to escape his guilt for one killing by planning another, by enthusiastically agreeing to Pylades' plot to murder Helen. In every version we feel the desperation with which he longs for release from memory and guilt.

In relation to female psychology Orestes is what Jungians would call Elektra's negative animus—she uses him to actualize her own aggressive fantasies. He is really poor material for her project. Childlike, malleable, and innocent, cut off from his mother at a tender age, he is still angry at having lost her and all too ready to follow a female's lead—and then lay the blame on her. Everyone seems to recognize that the energy for revenge is really Elektra's. Their grandfather Tyndareus, whom Orestes remembers as cherishing him like one of his own sons when he was little, after the matricide contemptuously addresses Orestes as a "thing," as but Elektra's pawn:

> It was *she,*
> that girl, who incited you against your mother,
> stuffing your ears day in and day out
> with her malice and venom, telling you her dreams
> of Agamemnon's ghost and what he said,
> tattling to you of your mother's adultery
> . . . .
> Yes, she worked on you
> until she set this whole house on fire
> with the arson of her malice[9]

As in "Hansel and Gretel," this sister and brother have really been deserted by both parents, but the abandonment by the mother feels the more unforgivable—especially to the daughter.

If I look at the relationship between Orestes and Elektra in terms of male psychology, I find confirmation of Freud's sense of the intimate connection between sisters and death. I see Elektra representing the denied death wish turned outward and taking the form of murderous aggression. Iphigenia, on the other hand, seems to represent the willing acceptance of one's own death, the discovery that one may come to terms with vulnerability and mortality and find oneself still alive. The reconnection with *this* sister is the necessary climax of Orestes' search for purification.

In his *Iphigenia in Tauris* Euripides shows how important Iphigenia and Orestes are to each other. As we have already noted, according to this play Iphigenia was not really killed at Aulis but spirited away from the funeral pyre and made the chief priestess of Artemis at Tauris. There she is responsible for the fearful sacrifices of human strangers to the awesome goddess. Despite the many intervening years, Iphigenia still dreams of her long-lost brother. As the play opens, she recalls a deathly dream in which she watched her childhood home fall to the ground with but one column left upright, but that one stood alive, a man with bright brown hair and breathing lips. In the dream she had reached toward this man and touched his forehead with the same fatal water with which here at Tauris she anoints the strangers condemned to die. She wakes understanding the dream as signifying Orestes' death. She shares with her maidens her nearly unbearable grief over the death of her only brother—who from childhood has thought *her* dead and whom she remembers only as a child at Klytemnestra's breast. She remembers herself as her mother's cherished firstborn child, remembers the joy with which her mother had identified with the daughter chosen to be Achilles' bride. As Iphigenia reflects on how differently it all turned out, on how she came to live beside this melancholy sea, wife of no man and mother of no child, we understand that for her Orestes is the child she never had. "I have loved him through all these lonely years." As she feels her sorrow over his faraway death, she wonders if her victims have sisters who mourn them.

In perfect counterpoint to this, when Orestes is brought before the priestess and knows that he must die, he cries, "I wish my sister's hand might tend my body." We are prepared then for the incomparable joy with which each will learn who the other is. "There is no language sweet enough to tell it. There is no joy like this. There never was." For Iphigenia to see Orestes still alive, to see the baby a grown man, is the beginning of a miracle. Orestes, too, has treasured memories of his long-lost sister through all the years. Elektra had told him so many stories, each of which he remembers; she had pointed out to him the tapestries Iphigenia had woven, her wedding gifts, the keepsakes in her room. Yet even in the midst of their joy, Iphigenia is afraid as she remembers the horrors of her family history, of her father's betrayal of her, of her own death. She cannot understand how Orestes could have sided with Agamemnon, how he could have killed her mother. Orestes acknowledges that he cannot explain; his deed was the unforgivable response to her unforgivable sin. He knows only that he has been sent by Apollo to bring the statue of Artemis stolen by the Taurians back to Greece and told that with the accomplishment of this deed, his unforgivable crime will be forgiven. As Orestes and Iphigenia (with the statue and with Pylades) make their escape, we recognize how each has rescued the other. We understand also that their bond is a recapitulation in the mortal world of the bond between Artemis and Apollo.

According to at least one tradition the news of Orestes and Iphigenia's safe return is long delayed in reaching Argos; instead a rumor comes to Elektra that her brother was killed by the Taurian priestess of Artemis who has since then come to serve the goddess at her shrine in Delphi. Elektra goes to Delphi with the intention of blinding her brother's supposed murderer, but Orestes intervenes and the two sisters are reconciled.

Orestes' fate is clearly intertwined with that of both sisters. Though the impulse for the matricide may have been Elektra's, it is Orestes who did the deed and who pays, whom the Furies pursue. As he and Elektra separate after Orestes' Argive trial, they expect never to see each other again. Orestes cries to her, "O my sister, these loving words, this last sweet embrace, is all we shall ever know in life of marriage and children." But he is mistaken. The Dioscuri appear to bring forgiveness to Elektra as Orestes' banishment begins; soon thereafter she marries Pylades, Orestes' "brother," and in time bears him two sons. Orestes, too, after suffering his inescapable punishment, is eventually purified. His terrible deed was also a necessary one; the generations-long curse comes to an end. Orestes is wed to another cousin, Helen's daughter, Hermione, and ends up as ruler of Mycenae, Argos, and Sparta, the most powerful monarch in the Peloponnesus.

Among the Mycenaeans the bond between sister and brother finally puts to an end the history of fratricide and adultery. The story closes not in tragedy but in reconciliation, with marriages and births. It is far otherwise in Thebes.

Yet the story of Antigone's devotion to her brother, Polyneices, was for the Greeks *the* story about the bond between sister and brother. The story focuses on *her* love for him. The myth's evocation of her consummate attachment may be a story men need to believe. It communicates that, from the male perspective the relation between sister and brother is the deepest of all human bonds (though for women the bond of sister to sister may be even more profound).

We see Antigone first as daughter/sister to Oedipus, as guide to his blind wandering, as companion in his death. (Oedipus saw in her courageous loyalty also the devotion of a brother/son.) She appears in *Oedipus at Colonus* as a Persephone figure, a guide toward the underworld, a psychopomp. She easily fits Freud's image of the sister as the goddess of death.

But it is in relation to Polyneices that her sisterly character is most powerfully revealed. Even at Colonus she implores their dying father, "Let *our* brother come here—for my sake. Remember your own father and what endless horror the rejection of sons by fathers sets into motion." But Oedipus cannot forgive his son's desertion and gives him only his terrible curse. Leaving, Polyneices begs his sisters, "If you find some way of getting home, give me a grave." Antigone begs her brother not to go back to Thebes with his mercenary army, begs him not to go toward his own death and their brother's, but Polyneices cannot bear to appear more cowardly than Eteocles and so shrugs off her plea.

When *Antigone* opens, it is all over: the war fought, both brothers dead, the edict against Polyneices' burial made public. This violation of the sacred right to ceremonial interment evokes Antigone's affirmation that the brother-sister bond is the most intimate, the most compelling, of all human bonds. She gives unforgettable expression to her fantasy of a relation with an other that releases the self from its unbearable solitude without violating its authenticity. Autonomy and perfectly concordant relationship are here—and only here—compatible. She envisions herself and Polyneices as deeply alike—and as different from all other humans by virtue of their dread incestuous parentage.[10] (I call it a fantasy because it seems important to notice that Antigone and Polyneices never *lived* this intimacy; she came closer to the realization of such accord with Oedipus.) Antigone is convinced that the kinship bond between siblings based on their common relationship to the mother, their origin in the same womb, transcends all other human and social obligations. In her confrontation with Creon, Antigone emphasizes that Polyneices was her *mother's* son. In response Creon insists on seeing Antigone only as her *father's* daughter.

The insistence on the primacy of the relation to the mother distinguishes Antigone from Elektra, who sees conjugal and paternal bonds as more important. (Antigone's putting familial duty over civic obedience also clearly separates her from Agamemnon, who chose the polis over his daughter.) But for Antigone the bond between siblings is even more sacred than that between mother and child. Perhaps inevitably in Oedipus' family, there are hints of an incestuous dimension to her love for Polyneices, not as anything lived but as a subliminal possibility. Immediately after speaking of him as her dearest one, as the brother of her heart, Antigone grieves, "never a marriage-bed, never a marriage-song for me." (Her love for Polyneices seems to have eclipsed even her relation to her fiance, Haemon, though his continued commitment to her costs him his life, and at the end of the play it is his corpse that is found lying on hers, not her brother's.)

In their interactions Creon stresses the differences between Eteocles and Polyneices. Antigone insists, *"Both* are brothers; in death that is all that matters." Creon represents a conception of human life that cannot come to terms with death, that seeks to bar underworld reality from the polis. Insisting that the dead body is simply a body, he is not afraid to subject Polyneices' corpse to what for the Greek religious imagination constituted the most horrible of fates: to be eaten by dog or bird. For Antigone this refusal of honor to the dead is itself a violation of life. To her it is self-evident that at death, not the deeds, but simply the human existence, signify. Ritual burial recognizes this human essence; nonburial denies our humanity, prevents access to the underworld, the realm of death, prevents our homecoming in the earth.

Antigone knows she *must* bury her brother. Unlike Oedipus, she commits her crime knowingly; like him she wants to *know.* She had wanted to see Oedipus' burial place and only very reluctantly accepts that this is forbidden by the gods. Now as she disobeys Creon's proclamation, she can bear to admit that she does not know whether the gods support her, she does not know if her own death will lead to a reunion with the already dead members of her doomed family. She can call on Dionysos, while admitting that she does not know if he will hear or respond.

At the end this most sisterly of souls (as Goethe called her) is radically alone. Her integrity as a human being is for her entirely dependent on her *being* a sister. In her conception this represents an ultimate bond that is not to be confused with intimacy in any ordinary sense. The brother and sister come from the same womb; together they reenter the womb of earth.

5. Tragic Sisters

In Greek mythology the two themes of mortality and sisterhood seem always to be closely intertwined. Because coming to love the sister—for females as well as for males—represents letting go of the mother, it is from the beginning rooted in an experience of loss and mourning. For a woman, the myths suggest, the relation to a sister involves the discovery of an otherness more subtle than that between daughter and mother and yet as inescapable. This, too, is a discovery of limitation, of finitude.

Before turning to the particular sisterly pairs that fascinated the dramatic poets, I want to consider more briefly some that we know of primarily from the epic poets and from later retellers of Greek myths such as Apollodorus and Ovid.

There are, for example, the two daughters of Perse and Helios (the sun god who sees everything): Circe and Pasiphaë. Both are spoken of as sorceresses in the late traditions, a covert indication of their divine origin, their more than human female powers. Carl Kerenyi speaks of Circe as a goddess of the periphery, whose lonely island lies only one day's journey from night. Alluringly beautiful and frighteningly powerful, she is a "hetaera of death" who transforms any man or woman who sets foot on her island into beast or stone. But when Odysseus comes to her island on his long journey home from Troy, she falls in love with him. After a year of lovemaking she sends him and his men on their way, directing Odysseus to the underworld, where alone he can learn how to find his way back to Ithaka.[1] According to one late tradition, when the son she bore Odysseus grows up she sends him in search of his father. Not recognizing Odysseus, the youth inadvertently kills him and then brings the body back to her for burial. Telemachus and Penelope come with him, and Circe ends up marrying Telemachus and Penelope, the "witch's" son.

Pasiphaë was married to Minos, king of Crete. In punishment

for her husband's failure to sacrifice a handsome bull to Poseidon, the queen falls passionately in love with the beast and gives birth to the ill-famed minotaur. Later, angered by Minos' many affairs, she bewitches him so that he impregnates his mistresses with poisonous vermin. One sister turns men into beasts; the other (with Daedalus' help—he builds a hollow wooden cow for her that she enters for her trysts with the bull) becomes a beast herself. Yet Pasiphaë was worshiped as a moon goddess on Crete, and one senses that Daedalus' artificial construction is a late rationalization. Originally perhaps Pasiphaë represented the self-transformative powers of the feminine, her sister the power of transforming others.

Pasiphaë has many human sons and two daughters, Ariadne and Phaedra. The most familiar tale about Ariadne represents her as a young maiden in love with Theseus, who helps him succeed in the dangerous task of entering the labyrinth, killing the minotaur, and finding his way back out. When he flees Crete and sails home toward Athens, he takes her with him but then leaves her behind on the island where they beach during the first night of the journey. Though some say that she committed suicide in grief over being abandoned, the earlier traditions represent her being rescued by Dionysos and becoming his wife. Indeed, there is much to suggest that, like her mother, Ariadne was in reality a powerful divinity in her own right. (She is visible in the sky as the constellation Corona Borealis.) Theseus may have been wiser than he knew to leave her behind. (Jason, less wise, as we noted in the last chapter, takes Ariadne's cousin Medea back to Greece with him.) The bride of Dionysos, she is a goddess of committed passion and undying love, a goddess of death, a goddess who gives birth in death. The adventure-loving Theseus was hardly her match.[2]

Years later when Theseus is ready to settle down as king of Athens and to arrange for a secure succession, he marries Ariadne's much younger sister, Phaedra. They spend a part of each year at Troezen where Theseus' grandfather still rules and where Hippolytus, Theseus' son by his dead Amazon queen, lives. This chaste youth is so exclusively devoted to his mother's goddess, Artemis, that scorned Aphrodite determines to take revenge. She causes Phaedra to fall as madly in love with her stepson as her mother had with the bull. Phaedra is ashamed of her passion but obsessed by it. Pitiably she approaches the young man, who, appalled, of course rejects her. Now quite mad, Phaedra kills herself and leaves a note for her husband in which she accuses Hippolytus of having raped her. Furious, Theseus curses his son and—before he discovers the youth's innocence—the curse is fulfilled: Hippolytus' horses are frightened by a bull that comes raging out of the sea; the chariot capsizes and kills him. The stories are all closely interwined, because, of course, the bull was sent by Poseidon.

Euripides' *Hippolytus* retells this story in all its tragic complexity but has little to say about the relation between Ariadne and Phaedra. In Mary Renault's modern recension of the Theseus myths,[3] Phaedra is presented as very aware of being Ariadne's younger sister, envious of her greater radiance, proud to have married the hero her sister had adored and lost. In Troezen, Phaedra, a minor goddess in her own world, is but a pawn—not only in the conflict between Artemis and Aphrodite, but also (this is Renault's emphasis) in the conflict between the old goddess-dominated world and the world of patriarchal order with which Theseus identifies. Nevertheless Phaedra ends up bringing the disasters to his house that Theseus thought he had avoided by leaving her sister on Naxos. Though Phaedra may be a *younger* sister, she is clearly a member of the same family, a daughter of Pasiphaë, a niece of Circe.

A sister story that Ovid tells to great effect concerns the two daughters of the Athenian king Pandion. He gives the older, Procne, in marriage to Tereus, a king of Thrace, as a reward for his support in a boundary dispute. After some years Procne pines for a visit from her sister, Philomela, and Tereus goes back to Athens to fetch her. As soon as he sets eyes on the beautiful younger daughter, he falls passionately in love with her. Unaware of this, Pandion, though he finds the thought of having both his daughters so far away painful, entrusts Philomela to Tereus' care. When they arrive in Thrace, Tereus takes the girl to a forest hut and rapes her. Philomela cries at him, "You have confounded all natural feeling, have tried to make me my sister's rival, her enemy. If I have the chance I will tell her the whole terrible story." To ensure that she cannot, Tereus cuts off her tongue. He locks her up in the hut and continues to visit and rape her. When he returns to his palace he tells his wife that her sister died on the voyage back from Athens.

But Philomela manages to weave a tapestry that tells the entire story and to have it secretly taken to Procne, who immediately decides on revenge. It is obvious to her that Tereus, not Philomela, is the guilty party. Pretending that she is planning to participate in a bacchic rite, she goes into the forest, finds the hut, frees her sister, and brings her back to the palace in disguise.

More horror comes as the two sisters decide how to take revenge against Tereus. Like Medea, Procne sacrifices her own son as the only act dramatic enough fully to communicate her rage at his father. Together she and Philomela kill the boy, Itys, and serve him to Tereus in a stew. When Tereus asks after the child, Philomela shows him the bloody severed head. Enraged, he takes after the women with a drawn sword. As they flee, Procne is turned into a nightingale and Philomela into a swallow.

This story poignantly expresses the situation of sisters oppressed by male power—betrayed, raped, rendered voiceless, grievously restricted in their capacity to retaliate—yet utterly committed to each other, able to find a way of communicating through a peculiarly womanly art (the weaving), courageously ready to risk the violation of universal taboos (against filicide and cannibalism). They live on as the nightingale, whose song represents love and endless yearning, and the swallow, the migratory bird that represents spring and rebirth.[4]

The inner connection between sisterhood and tragedy is clearly evident in Thebes, the birthplace of Dionysos (and in that sense of tragedy itself). The city was founded by Kadmos, a greatgrandson of Zeus, who was wedded to Harmonia, the daughter of Ares and Aphrodite. Born to this unique marriage between a goddess of love and a mortal were four daughters: Semele, Agave, Autonoe, and Ino. The stories associated with these sisters are without exception tragic tales.

Semele was the third oldest; but because it is her fate that so largely shapes that of her sisters, it seems most appropriate to begin with her. She is one of the beautiful mortal women with whom Zeus becomes sexually involved. Her proud boasts about the affair lead her sisters to taunt that she is concealing a liaison with some disreputable mortal under the cloak of this story about a divine lover; they persuade Hera to punish Semele for her temerity. Disguised as a kindly old gossip, Hera gets Semele to confide in her and then persuades the maiden to ask Zeus to come to her in his true form, the form in which he comes to his divine bride. Zeus warns Semele that her request is foolishly dangerous, but she insists. When he comes to make love to her in the shape of a fiery lightning bolt, the young woman is burnt to death—but she is six months pregnant with Zeus' child, and the god cannot bear to lose the babe as well as the mother. He sends Hermes to cut the still-living fetus out of her womb and has it sewn into his own thigh. Three months later Dionysos is born. When he is grown, this young god finds his way into the underworld, rescues Semele from Hades, and makes her a goddess.

But in the period immediately after her death, her sisters spread the rumor that she was killed by Zeus for falsely claiming that her bastard son was his child. Nonetheless they hide young Dionysos from the still vengeful Hera and help to raise him. Thus they have made themselves liable to punishment by Zeus, by Dionysos, and by Hera. No wonder their lot is not an easy one.

Autonoe's son, Actaeon, is turned into a stag and devoured by his own hounds as punishment for having accidentally seen Artemis naked bathing in a pond with her nymphs. Devastated by his death, Autonoe separates from her husband and dies alone in a remote desolate village.

When Dionysos returns to Thebes as an adult, Agave joins the maenads, who participate in the wild orgies celebrated in honor of the god on the mountaintop outside the city. In her frenzied madness, she kills her own son Pentheus, the self-consciously puritanical king of Thebes, who has been enticed to go spy on the celebrants. Agave tore the youth (whom she took for a lion cub) into bits with her own hands and teeth—thereby recapitulating the dismemberment suffered by Dionysos at the hands of the Titans. Later, so one story goes, Agave kills her second husband so that her ancient exiled father can have her husband's throne.

Ino had protected the infant Dionysos from Hera by disguising him as a girl. Like Agave, she joins the maenads when he reappears in Thebes as an adult god. In gratitude for her nursing of him when he was a defenseless child, Dionysos aids her in her struggles against her stepchildren by driving them mad and then protects her from being executed for her plots. Later, however, Hera (still angry at Ino's nursing Dionysos) drives Ino and her husband insane. In their madness, they kill their own children: the father shoots the older son, taking him for a deer; Ino boils the younger one and then leaps off a cliff with the boy in her arms. Ino herself does not die; she becomes a minor goddess worshiped by sailors, Leucothea, the White Goddess.

All four sisters lose their sons. Envious of the sister loved by a god, the other three wanted to deny the divinity of her son and thus the divinity of what he represents—passion. Though their stories are tragic, except for Euripides' *Bacchae* in which Agave has a prominent role, there are no surviving tragedies written about them. Therefore we do not have available to us the dramatic representation of the interplay between character and fate, of the inner meaning of their relationships with one another, that the tragedians supply.

For a later pair of Theban sisters, Antigone and Ismene, whose story seized the imagination of Sophokles, we have an intimate, deeply compelling representation of sisterly bonding. The lifelong relationship between Antigone and Ismene is shown as revealing its essence at a moment of crisis when childhood issues of identification and differentiation reappear.

Antigone *is* a sister—in a way that makes her relationship to both brother and sister centrally important. She and Ismene are bound together by their incestuous origin; their kinship is an outrage that separates them from all others. Thus they are so closely connected as to be almost fused. This differentiates their relationship from that of Elektra and Chrysothemis (which we will consider further on), in which Chrysothemis can more adequately be seen as a pale shadow of her older sister. The relationship between Antigone and Ismene is tense with the

struggle between the longing for fusion and the painful realization of differentiation. It communicates the dynamics of relationship to the closest other—who is nonetheless other.

Steiner sees the chorus in Greek tragedy as the late vestige of
a time in human experience when our consciousness was not
yet individualized, when primal fusion was an experienced reality. In Sophokles' drama the painful move toward a more individuated consciousness is powerfully enacted. I know how strong
the nostalgic longing for a sisterhood that might rediscover this
primal unity is in me. Adrienne Rich invokes this longing in a
beautiful forward–looking image:

> the secret revolution!
>   that two women can meet
> no longer as cramped sharers
> of a bitter mutual secret
> but as two eyes in one brow
> receiving at one moment
> the rainbow of the world.[5]

Antigone begins by seeing herself and Ismene as "two eyes in
one brow"; her discovery of this as illusion is heartbreaking.

When Oedipus is banished, Antigone accompanies him into
exile and Ismene stays in Thebes, but as their "faithful out-
post"—not like their brothers, who seem all too ready to regard
their father as dead and to seize the throne he was forced to
relinquish. When the dying Oedipus and Antigone arrive at
Colonus, Ismene appears to join them. Until then Oedipus has
been addressing Antigone as daughter, but now, as he embraces
both, he is so aware of *their* sisterhood that he recalls they are
his sisters as well and so addresses them, "My children, my
sisters."

Although in this last play of Sophokles Ismene appears somewhat self-absorbed—at first more occupied with her troubles in
getting to Colonus than with what is happening with her father
and later, after his death, so involved in her own grief as to be
almost oblivious to anyone else—she is nevertheless seen as a
clearly devoted and loyal daughter. Yet even in this representation she is less daring, more obedient, more conventional than
her sister. When Antigone wants to see her father's burial place,

Ismene immediately retorts, "But it's not permitted," as though that obviously settled the matter.

In Aeschylus' *Seven Against Thebes* the absolute, pure formal balance of the alternating dirge that Ismene and Antigone recite over their brothers' dead bodies speaks its own clear message. When Creon's edict against the burial of Polyneices is announced, Antigone voices defiance and leads those determined to mourn the dishonored brother; Ismene follows her but says nothing. Thus eloquently, chastely, Aeschylus communicates their closeness, their difference.

In Sophokles' *Antigone* the tension between them becomes focal. The play opens with Antigone saying, *"Sister."* (The Greek is an even more intense and essentially untranslatable evocation of the intimacy of their union: Fagles writes, "My own flesh and blood—dear sister"; Braun, "Let me see your face, my own, only sister"; Steiner suggests a literal version would be more like, "My sister, my face," as though they shared only one face between them.)[6] Antigone reminds Ismene of their common heritage, their common suffering; she articulates her anger at Creon giving orders "to you and me" to leave their brother unwept, untombed, and her determination to disobey.

Ismene replies, "But it's forbidden." She rehearses all the horrors their family has already suffered and asks if they are not sufficient. She says she will obey Creon and ask forgiveness of those below the earth, confident it will be granted. "What can I do?" she asks. "We must remember that we two are women." She has learned that "wild and futile action" makes no sense. To her mind Antigone yearns for impossible, lost modes of total kinship.

Antigone responds, "After that, I wouldn't want your help even if you offered it. *I'*ll dare the crime of piety."

The inner significance of the fusion implicit in Antigone's first word is radically different from that between the fairy-tale figures Snow White and Rose Red, because here we are given access to the profound pain that its loss, the discovery of difference, engenders. Here we feel the anguish of the consequent isolation. Ismene can from the beginning so easily speak a singular "I," can refer to Polyneices as "my" brother, can ignore the mysteries of blood. The "I" that Antigone is forced to speak as she realizes Ismene's otherness becomes a sign of solitude and alienation.

After Antigone's attempt to bury Polyneices, Creon accuses both sisters of the deed. Ismene is willing to accept responsibility, but Antigone refuses her any involvement. Ismene pleads to her sister, "Am I outside your fate?" and Antigone responds, "Yes." Ismene weeps, wondering, "What life is there for me to live without her?"

Sophokles' presentation allows us to appreciate both perspectives, Antigone's and Ismene's. Steiner speaks of Ismene as "the most beauteous measure of the ordinary." Ismene's sanity shows up the mad obsessiveness of both her sister and her uncle. Like Chrysothemis she is the cautious sister. But, as we'll see, Chrysothemis' reservations are based on her sense of her own weakness; she does not doubt the justice of Elektra's position but sees herself as too cowardly actively to support it. Ismene's doubts reflect her commitment to a morality different from Antigone's. Her words make apparent the bitter core of Antigone's motivations: the hatred of Creon, the egotistical pride that leads her to deny her kinship to Ismene. Antigone is seen not to be as all-loving as she claims to be.

Ismene counterposes her own womanliness to what she perceives as Antigone's masculinity. In Sophokles' plays, others, too, speak of Antigone's masculine aspect: Oedipus appreciatively, when he finds her more manly than her disloyal brothers; Creon pejoratively and with a measure of fear, "I am no man and she the man instead." At one point Antigone even uses the masculine "I" in speaking of herself. Yet Antigone also has specifically feminine feelings; she voices her deeply painful regrets over the virginity she will never lose, the children she will never have. Her fundamental conviction that kinship bonds supersede all civically imposed duty is in Greek mythology typically associated with the age-old matriarchal perspective, with the values the Erinyes uphold, with chthonic religiosity. Antigone's suicide by hanging is, according to the conventions of Greek mythology, a paradigmatically female response to the unbearable horrors of life. It recalls the deaths of Ariadne, of Phaedra, and most particularly of Antigone's mother, Jocasta.

Antigone ends up vehemently denying to Ismene the very

sense of irrevocable kinship that motivates her to bury Polyneices. Her sense of drastic estrangement leads her to betray,
with respect to her sister, the very heart of her own deepest
convictions. The one so intensely pulled toward human inter-
fusion becomes the most solitary, the most anarchically egotistical of persons. Antigone feels herself to be absolutely alone.
Not at home with either the living or the dead, she may be
exiled even more radically than Oedipus, may be even more
unwept than Polyneices. Having completely severed her relation
to Ismene, she still hopes, but without assurance, to rejoin the
rest of her doomed family in Hades. She feels herself to be the
last of them all.

But Ismene survives. Although from Antigone's perspective it
is precisely Ismene's overvaluation of survival that annuls her
life, from her own she represents a feminine insistence on the
importance of ongoing life and the continuity of human generations. These sisters represent two essentially opposed morali-
ties. They are not really rivals; nor is one given strength and
the other relegated weakness. Each in her own way is equally
powerful and fully female. Though as close to each other as
two humans can be, they are fundamentally *other*.

The other most compelling explorations of the theme of sisterhood in the Greek tragic tradition focus on Helen and Klytemnestra and Klytemnestra's daughters, Iphigenia, Elektra, and
Chrysothemis.

Helen and Klytemnestra were both daughters of Leda, though
Helen was fathered by a god, Zeus (she was his only mortal
daughter), and Klytemnestra by Leda's mortal husband, Tyndareus, the king of Sparta. There is another tradition that their
mother is really Nemesis, the goddess of retribution, who laid
an egg that Leda protected until the girls were hatched from
it; this tradition sees all that happens in the life of the sisters as
determined by the roles they are destined to play in the fulfillment of the curse laid on their Pelopid husbands. The fate of
the daughters is also sometimes tied to Tyndareus' having of-
fended Aphrodite by failing to offer the appropriate sacrifice;
this tradition notes that it is as a swan, Aphrodite's bird, that

Zeus makes love to Leda. Yet these traditions that subordinate their stories, make them simply pawns in a world where the really important figures are male, are unconvincing. Helen and Klytemnestra are too clearly female figures possessed of uncanny, daemonic, perhaps divine, power. The clumsy attempts to reduce their stature by representing them as instruments of the gods' revenge simply show that their lives are indeed godtouched, that their stories have an awesome archetypal authority that the notion of fatedness helps to express. Certainly their daughters' fate is deeply disturbing to both parents. Leda kills herself after Helen runs off to Troy. Tyndareus is deeply ashamed of both his daughters, though he also continues to love both: he welcomes Helen back from Troy; he brings flowers for Klytemnestra's grave.

The two sisters are obsessed with each other. They serve as mirrors to each other—though each seeks vehemently to deny any likeness between them. In Jungian terms each is clearly shadow to the other. Their relation highlights the negative dimensions of the sister bond, perhaps because both are so largely defined by their relationships with men.

The lives of these two sisters keep them involved with brothers—their own, Kastor and Polydeukes, and the two they marry, Agamemnon and Menelaus. (Before their marriages to these brothers, however, each had an earlier lover: Helen, Theseus; and Klytemnestra, Tantalus, a son of Thyestes. And, according to some traditions, each had already lost a child: Helen had had to give up the daughter Theseus fathered to be raised by her sister; Klytemnestra had had to watch Agamemnon beat out the brains of her child by Tantalus.) Agamemnon is forced on Klytemnestra; she begins as a passive figure, whereas Helen chooses Menelaus for his wealth and power. The two sisters differentiate, discover their own adult identities, as they turn away from the Mycenaean brothers who are their husbands. Both turn to lovers when their husbands leave them. Helen runs off with Paris while Menelaus is in Crete at his grandfather's funeral. Klytemnestra begins her affair with Aegisthus in response to Agamemnon's going to Troy. When Helen lets herself be abducted by Paris, she embraces the passivity that henceforward marks her life. When Klytemnestra takes her husband's familial enemy to her bed, she enters upon that active direction of her own life that thereafter characterizes her.

Both Menelaus and Agamemnon end up as victims of their wives and are remembered in the epics and tragedies primarily as husbands. The women give them their immortality. Menelaus remains the man who lost his wife—even after he regains her. He is a consort not a hero. Agamemnon is remembered as the man killed by his wife.

Helen is woman as object, the symbol of the goal of romantic quest and heroic struggle. Probably the Helen of Greek myth was first a goddess like Selene, associated with the moon and the theme of abduction and rape, who is "reduced" to mortal status in association with the establishment of the Olympian pantheon. Even in the later traditions her immortality continues to shine through the stories told about her, despite their often negative perspective. She confers glory and immortality on the heroes who die for her at Troy, both Trojan and Greek. Her relation to Aphrodite is subtly shifting: is she the goddess's pawn or her embodiment? Like an archaic fertility goddess, she is always being raped—and rescued. When Theseus abducts her in her youth, her brothers, the Dioscuri, liberate her; when Paris takes her to Troy, the sons of Atreus (with a good deal more effort) fight to bring her back.[7]

The central event in Helen's life is clearly her abduction by Paris and the consequent decade-long war. In Euripides' *Helen* she excuses herself for having no real loyalty to either side by reminding us that she was "conceived in an act of treachery." Helen *never* takes responsibility for any of her deeds; over and over again she says: "It was the god"; "It was the goddess"; or "It was all Menelaus' fault for leaving me helpless and alone in Sparta while he went off to Crete." Again and again she tells us, "I was the bride of force." Helen, that is, herself adopts the objectified view of herself.

Some kinds of victimization are obviously harder for women to resist than others. Klytemnestra has a husband who abuses and betrays her, who is directly responsible for the murder of two of her children—and in the end she rejects the role of victim. Helen remains victimized by her bewitching beauty, by her power over men. That the beauty which fascinates and arouses envy is also a curse is something she occasionally glimpses—"I wish that like a picture I had been rubbed out and done again, made plain, without this loveliness"—and quickly forgets.

That Helen lives in a fantasy world is beautifully correlative with the fancy of Stesichorus (adopted by Euripides for his *Helen*) that the war was fought for naught, for a fantasy, that Helen never was in Troy but rather spent the whole ten years captive in Egypt. *This* Helen says, "It wasn't me they fought over but my name. For a cloud, for nothing, all that dying." The fantasy clearly suits a Helen anxious to live on afterward as though none of it had ever happened, to imagine herself with all the virtues of Penelope.

Actually, of course, Helen abandoned not only her husband but also her daughter, Hermione, who was raised by Klytemnestra while Helen was in Troy. (There is also the tradition that Iphigenia was really Helen's bastard daughter and that she, too, was given to Klytemnestra to bring up.) Hermione's anger at her mother's desertion is deep, though unlike Elektra she never gives it more than verbal expression. Eventually (after a disastrous first marriage) Hermione marries her cousin Orestes: "It wouldn't be easy to marry outside the family."

The relationship between the sisters persists even after Klytemnestra's death. Helen and Menelaus come home to Sparta after their long journey back from Troy on the very day Orestes is condemned to death for murdering Klytemnestra. When Menelaus refuses to offer his brother's son any support, Orestes in mad outrage unsuccessfully attempts to kill Helen, too. But far from feeling any identification with her sister or any grief over her death, Helen is furious at how Klytemnestra's reputation as a murderess will now besmirch her own name.

Yet she comes to Elektra as though devastated by Klytemnestra's death and Elektra's orphaned state: "You poor girl, and still unmarried, too. . . . I know it was Apollo's fault. . . . But poor Klytemnestra, my only sister. And to think I sailed for Troy without even seeing her. Some god must have driven me mad. And now she is gone, and I am the only one left to mourn her." (As Elektra observes, Helen is as usual busily rewriting history.) She continues, "Elektra, would you go to your mother's grave for me?" To which Elektra not surprisingly responds, "But she was *your* sister." So Helen sends Hermione instead, telling her to implore Klytemnestra to be gracious to the loving sister who sends these gifts. Again Elektra acutely and bitterly notes, "The same old Helen—just a tiny clip of curls."

Though Helen condemns Klytemnestra as an adulteress and a murderess, the same labels clearly apply to her. Pylades explicitly tells her that to his mind she is every bit as much a murderer as her sister—more, when one considers the many men, Greek and Trojan, who died because of her. (In Euripides' *Elektra,* Helen herself confesses to being just as much a mother's murderer as is her niece.)

As the poet says, "All Greece hates Helen—and all Troy." Especially the women: in the larger sense, Helen has no sisters. Andromache accuses her, "Cry it aloud: Zeus never was your father, but you were born a pestilence to all Greeks and the world beside." Menelaus is mocked for his obsession with his Helen. "You should have left the slut in Troy, paid her to stay away." Hecuba tells Menelaus she cannot understand why he does not kill Helen rather than her. "All this came to pass for the way one woman chose a man." To Helen she says, "You worked hard—not to be a better woman, but to be always on the winning side. A true woman would have hanged herself."

Helen does, indeed, end up hanged—not by her own agency but by that of Greek women still angry years later about the men killed in the senseless war fought over her. Driven out of Sparta by Menelaus' sons after his death, she fled to Rhodes. There a group of women dressed as Erinyes hanged her on a tree.

According to the tales, Helen was Zeus' child and Klytemnestra but the daughter of a mortal king, and there is much in the traditions about the relationship between them to suggest that Klytemnestra always felt herself overshadowed by her more beautiful, more divine sister. Yet Klytemnestra, too, was god-possessed and, like her sister, had a cult devoted to her. Kassandra recognized this, saw in Klytemnestra the same mad, god-driven energy that pulsed in the maenads, that coursed through Agave. It is not difficult, after all, to discover in Klytemnestra's murder of Agamemnon the age-old pattern whereby the old king is ritually sacrificed so that the new may take his place. The slaying is done by the stranger, the intruding successor— and by the goddess. Through participation in this ancient cult the deceased ruler is immortalized—as Agamemnon is immortalized (by Homer, by Aeschylus, in our memories these many centuries later) as the king killed by Klytemnestra.[8] (The traditions differ, of course, as to whether the determination behind the killing is primarily that of Klytemnestra or of Aegisthus. Surely he had adequate motivation of his own: Agamemnon had deposed his father, murdered his brother, stolen the throne he might otherwise have inherited. For him the whole affair with Klytemnestra might have been but part of a complicated plot of revenge. But in Acschylus we sense that Klytemnestra truly loved him and he her—and in any case that both were involved in the deed seems to be the most compelling way of telling the tale.) The imagery in Aeschylus' *Agamemnon* makes this ritual dimension evident. The king's death becomes a sacrificial one as he knowingly walks on the crimson carpet reserved for offerings to the gods. He dies in requital for the crime of Atreus—and for the sacrifice of Iphigenia.

Klytemnestra kills her husband—as her long ago ancestress Hypermnestra refused to kill hers. Each chooses to make her own decisions about how to respond to what the Fates send as her destiny. Klytemnestra is the subject of her life, an active agent.

She was, as I have already reported, married first to a son of Thyestes. When Agamemnon kills her husband and child, her brothers, the Dioscuri, attack him—but Tyndareus, their father and hers, intervenes. Tyndareus not only rescues Agamemnon but marries his daughter to her spouse's murderer. Though it was a forced marriage, all the traditions agree that to begin with Klytemnestra was a faithful wife. When Klytemnestra comes to Aulis, proud that her daughter is to be Achilles' bride, and learns that instead she is to be killed in a ritual sacrifice, she cannot forgive her husband. She warns Agamemnon of the likely consequences of what he purposes. "Don't force me to become a woman of evil, to betray you." She tells him that none of his other children could ever forgive him (and I weep when I remember how wrong she is, how readily Elektra forgave). In

Aeschylus' *Agamemnon* Klytemnestra speaks bitterly of their sacrificed daughter, whose fate Agamemnon saw as entirely in *his* hands: "*His* own child, *my* dearest birthpang."

Klytemnestra's story has almost always been told from the male perspective, from the perspective of the victorious, the patriarchal, side. We are familiar with the hostile portrait of her, the laudatory one of Orestes—yet even as the story has come down to us it is easy for us to understand her anger at Helen, and at Agamemnon, who killed two of her children—and was unfaithful. In Euripides' *Elektra* Klytemnestra says the infidelity was the decisive wound—not Iphigenia but Chryseis and Kassandra—the shame of being replaced and the unfairness of being condemned for *her* adultery when men never seem to be blamed at all for theirs. She is furious about the double standard: Agamemnon would never have been willing to sacrifice Orestes to save Menelaus.

Aeschylus gives us a Klytemnestra with "the mind and counsel of a man"—counterposed both against her weak consort, Aegisthus, who "like a woman waited out the war at home," and against Agamemnon, who protests that her welcome pampers him as though he were a woman. As a human woman Klytemnestra is condemned for actions and attributes that in her divine counterpart, Athene, are praised. That we can see this in the poet's language (which at points subverts his plot) suggests that the poet, too, recognized her grandeur: the tragedy of a powerful woman confined to a role, that of the wife in a patriarchal world, too small for her.[9]

There are some intimations in the tragedies that Klytemnestra has sisters in that wider sense in which Helen has none, that other women have respect and sympathy for her. Hecuba is awed when she hears Klytemnestra's deed prophesied: "She would never do it!" In Euripides' *Trojan Women* Kassandra acknowledges a secret kinship with Klytemnestra; she foresees that Agamemnon's marriage to her will destroy him. She is prepared then to go to her own death—triumphant.[10]

Though married first, though willing to bring up her sister's first, illegitimate child in her own respectable household, though really the one who chose Menelaus as her sister's husband—though in so many ways this twin took on the role of older

sister, in another sense, she may always have felt herself out-
shone by Helen's divine birth and unmatched beauty. Clearly
her sister was always there, an invisible presence at every moment of Klytemnestra's life. At times, as in Euripides' *Iphigenia
at Aulis*, she is ready to see everything as "that slut's" fault, that
slut whose daughter is safe in Klytemnestra's palace. At another
time, in another play, Klytemnestra is unwilling to have the guilt
so wholly laid on Helen as to exonerate Agamemnon. In the
Agamemnon when the chorus accuses Helen

> for the multitudes, for the thousand lives
> you killed under Troy's shadow,
> you alone, to shine in man's memory
> as blood flowers never to be washed out

Klytemnestra responds:

> No, be not so heavy . . .
> neither turn all wrath against Helen
> for men dead, that she alone killed
> all those Danaan lives.[11]

As I rehearse their stories I am impressed again by how much
alike these sisters are—and by how neither can bear to admit
it. Acknowledgment would mean having to understand themselves in a much more critical (and responsible) way. Both recognize that in some way their cousin Penelope, with whom they
were raised, serves as a norm of female integrity in relation to
which they fall short. Penelope remains faithful to a husband
absent almost twice as long as Agamemnon; she successfully
puts off her unwanted suitors; her son remains loyal. She represents the home to which most of the heroes will never return
but that in retrospect they would have chosen over the glory
conferred upon them by dying in the war over Helen.

The mythical traditions suggest that Iphigenia and Elektra
were both deeply influenced by their sense of the relation between their mother and Helen. Their own sense of the sisterly
bond emerges in conscious and unconscious response to how it
is modeled by the older women. It is almost as though they hope
to avoid repeating the same conflict-ridden pattern of relationship and so adopt the familiar strategies of de-identification to

defuse rivalry and assure differentiation—but they do so at the cost of intimacy and empathy. (Their mother's and aunt's sexuality—how much it cost them and all who came in contact with them—may also have robbed them of the capacity to enjoy their own.)

Again there is a tradition that though sisters, they do not really have the same parentage—for Iphigenia may be Helen's child. Like Helen she is worshiped as a goddess, as the goddess to whom her life is sacrificed, in this case not Aphrodite but Artemis. (Whereas Elektra is the clearly mortal sister, though as with Klytemnestra that is not after all quite as clear as at first appears; her being named after two goddesses, the Elektra who is the mother of Iris and the Harpies, and another Elektra, a paramour of Zeus who is one of the Pleiades, may signify that she, too, has some divine status.) Again, there is an active sister, Elektra, and a more passive one, Iphigenia. One, Iphigenia, is a mother's daughter; her sister identifies with the father.

Iphigenia's name, which means "she who governs births mightily," implies her relation to Artemis, the goddess of childbirth. Chosen as the purest sacrifice, she embodies the goddess's virginal chastity. She is the eldest daughter, as she reminds Agamemnon in pleading for her life: "I was the first to call you father." Though Klytemnestra dotes on her firstborn child, she accepts that at least as an adolescent Iphigenia seems to love her father more. Learning of her father's decision to have her sacrificed, Iphigenia implores him, "Be mine only." As she discovers him to be unyielding, as she realizes that he is determined to put his glory as leader of the Greeks above his devotion to his family, she still seeks to put more blame on Helen than on him. She came to Aulis as to a wedding and learns she is to be married to death. By putting a heroic construction on her death, by seeing herself as a savior of Greece, by making herself a willing sacrifice, she comes to terms with her destiny. She tells Achilles, "I want to save men, not be like Helen who has them die for her." To her mother she says, "Don't weep for me; through me you'll be remembered gloriously." Her last message to her sisters at home is, "Don't wear mourning." As she goes to her death, she begs Klytemnestra to take care of Orestes and not to hate Agamemnon.

As far as her family knows, she dies there at Aulis: a bride of death, a silent goddess. In reality she is rescued by Artemis and taken to Tauris to serve her as chief priestess. Then follow the long years of isolation. When Orestes finds her, she seems to have displaced all her anger at Agamemnon onto Menelaus and Helen—yet her real sympathy is clearly with Klytemnestra. She cannot understand how Orestes could have killed their mother. Through the years of separation she has continued to feel sistered by Elektra. "Tell me about Elektra," she cries to Orestes, "I cannot wait." She is clearly deeply moved to learn how Elektra has kept her memory alive, how she taught Orestes to love the absent sister whose childhood weavings, innocent keepsakes, wedding gifts, still filled the palace at Mycenae.

Elektra, though she has spent all those years since the Greek ships sailed from Aulis at home, has also in a sense been taken out of her life—for she has spent the whole time *waiting*, waiting for her father to return. She is so put off by her mother's adultery that her own ongoing life, her own female existence, seems to have been taken from her. She cannot bear to watch Aegisthus sit on her father's throne, wear her father's clothes. Finally the waiting is over, Agamemnon returns—and is murdered. Elektra sends Orestes away for safekeeping and returns to her waiting, waiting now for her brother to grow up and return to her.

Meanwhile Elektra is imprisoned by Aegisthus, who fears she might bear a son who would contest his children's accession to the throne. Although he weds her to the old peasant who serves as her guard, he ensures that she will remain a virgin. In Euripides' *Elektra* she piteously protests her own lonely sleep, while her mother "breeds new children in Aegisthus' bed," "while my mother rolls in her bloody bed and plays at love with a stranger." Elektra lives only in the past. Fatherless, husbandless, childless, cut off from her mother and sister, she has no present. Consumed by her loneliness and hate, by her hope for revenge, Elektra cries, "I'll never stop mourning, though I know it's madness." Elektra's anger that her mother still has babies while she has none inspires the deceit whereby, in this play, she entices Klytemnestra to her death. She sends word that she is in childbirth and wants her mother by her.

Elektra's passionate preference for the father seems clearly motivated by her anger at her mother's abandonment. "Women save all their love for lovers, not for children," she cries. (We might note here that Hermione, by contrast, feels she receives from her aunt the nurturant and sympathetic mothering her own mother did not provide.) Though many years have passed, Elektra is still envious of the devotion Klytemnestra showed to Iphigenia. "Why not give that motherly love to me when my sister was killed? You still love the dead one most." Yet a moment later she will accuse Klytemnestra of using Iphigenia's death as a screen, a false excuse for turning to Aegisthus: "You started primping the day my father left." "You were the only Greek woman to rejoice when the Trojans were winning, and you loved it when Helen's reputation was blackened. So why didn't you use that as an opportunity to keep your purity in contrast to her shame?"

Although Klytemnestra maintains that Elektra had always adored her father "as some girls always do," she nonetheless feels betrayed by the persistence of the preference after Iphigenia is killed. To her mind it is Elektra who disgraces the family. "Your father, always your father. But what of your sister?" Elektra's reply: "Daddy had to do it—for Greece, not for his brother, not for Helen. Don't use my sister as an excuse for your adultery."

But she is more like her mother than she cares to admit. They stir up the Furies in one another whenever they meet. Elektra speaks angrily about women who assume the powers that belong to men: "What perversion when the woman is the master." Yet she dominates Orestes every bit as much as Klytemnestra dominates Aegisthus. In both instances it is the woman who takes the active role in urging murder, though both need men to help them with the deed itself. When Elektra and Orestes have accomplished their killing, when Klytemnestra lies dead before her, Elektra is at last free to feel her love—and her guilt: "A girl flaming in hurt I marched against the mother who bore me, the one I loved and could not love," Euripides has her say.

Puzzlement at the intensity of Elektra's consuming hatred of her mother is voiced by the chorus in Sophokles' *Elektra:* "But your sisters, Chrysothemis and Iphianassa suffered the same loss . . . " Sophokles counterposes Elektra's character to that of

Chrysothemis, her timid, sensible, and unattractive younger sister. This sister's name means "pale justice"; it seems to suit her perfectly. She does not contest the legitimacy of Elektra's purpose but foresees how such a resolution will only lead to further violence. She admits her own cowardice and weakness: "I must make my voyage with lowered sails." How she wishes that their family could just be like everyone else's.

Elektra accuses her, "You just follow Mother's lead, nothing is your own. When you could be daughter to the best of fathers, you choose instead to be a mother's daughter." But Chrysothemis is confident, "*My* father will have pardon for me." She wants to help Elektra, yet also stay free of guilt. "If I can help at all I will not refuse, but your plan is too reckless. Remember, you're a woman. Please—don't make things worse." She agrees to offer a sacrifice at Agamemnon's grave imploring his blessing; despite the "impropriety," she runs to tell Elektra of Orestes' return. But Elektra denies her: "Who are you to bring me good news?"

The tragedians give us no scenes of direct interaction between Elektra and the sister she does not deny, Iphigenia. That relationship is lived *through* Orestes. It is he who communicates to Iphigenia how Elektra kept her memory alive; it is he who hears Iphigenia's loving inquiry about her sister's fate; it is he who reconciles them before the Artemis shrine at Delphi. As I reflect on this I recall Freud's words about how two women who love the same man may really love one another.

I see in the tragedies' representations of sisters, patterns I recognize—and disavow—and then have to acknowledge as all too familiar after all. Again, the portrayal of brotherly relationships seems simpler. Fraternal bonds take the form of the Dioskuri's undying love *or* of the Atreides' unremitting hatred. (Though I recognize the relevance of *that* portrayal to my experience, also—I know what it is like to feel that two sisters are destined to have identical fates and somehow at the same time to believe that their lives are intertwined in such a way as to guarantee that if one is happy, the other must suffer. As we women live it, the alternatives seem to become simultaneously valid truths—the love and the hate are both present and if not sorted through issue in envy, guilt, paralysis.)

The stories about sisters bring the ambiguity and complexity into the foreground. It becomes almost impossible to decide where our sympathies or trust should fall. Is Antigone or Ismene right? Are Helen and Klytemnestra evil, death-bringing women or powerful female figures inevitably experienced as destructive in a male-dominated world? Must Elektra kill the mother who dominates her life?

I recognize the truth of the *intensity* of these sisterly bonds and of the lifelong *persistence* of that intensity. I recognize the pain in Antigone's discovery of Ismene's unalterable otherness—and the self-evident simplicity of Ismene's sense of her distinctness. I recognize the many affinities between Helen and Klytemnestra—and understand very well why they would deny them. I understand why Iphigenia and Elektra might choose to construct a safety zone separating them from each other—and bemoan its cost. I suffer for the self-wounding, narrowly constricted range of possible action that Philomela and Procne cannot escape in their efforts to stay true to one another. I, too, recognize—as all of us must—what it is like to feel oneself caught (as so many of these sisters did) in inherited patterns from which we seem powerless to extricate ourselves.

6. Divine Sisters—and Biblical Brothers

Although initially disappointed that Greek mythology offered no goddesses to model the sister bond, I have come to appreciate its representations of sisterhood as experienced by mortal women as a greater gift than the one initially sought. But after my immersion in these tragic tales, I remembered that, of course, there *are* sistered goddesses—not in the Greek traditions but in many other mythic systems. I knew it would be just as foolhardy to attempt to survey all mythic systems as it would have been to seek to examine all folklore traditions. Nevertheless it does seem relevant to look at those other mythologies that have most directly and deeply influenced Western culture—the mythologies of the ancient Near East, of Sumer, Egypt, and Israel. Sumer and Egypt provide an understanding of sisterhood I find even more profound than that given by Greece. Alternately, the Hebrew Bible depicts brotherly interaction as perhaps the most paradigmatic of all human bonds—and almost ignores sisterly bonds.

These traditions have less often been explored by either depth psychologists or feminists than have the Greek—although the Mesopotamian world has long fascinated scholars interested in the transition from small-scale, matrifocal, goddess-worshiping communities to the archaic patriarchal state. From Merlin Stone's ground-breaking 1976 study, *When God Was a Woman,* to Gerda Lerner's recent *The Creation of Patriarchy,* feminist scholars have found in Sumer the most telling clues to the disappearance of a world where women were accorded value equal to that given men.[1]

Even when I was in school forty years ago, we learned that according to the Babylonian creation epic, the *Enuma Elish,* the world as we know it, its physical landscape and human inhabitants, was fashioned from the blood and dismembered guts of the first divine being, the goddess Tiamat, after she was killed by her upstart grandson, Marduk. I remember, too, how fascinated I was to learn when I got to graduate school how the Genesis account of creation is modeled after the Babylonian story, how that watery chaos, "the deep," *tehom,* over which the biblical God hovers as he begins creating is linguistically related to the ancient serpent goddess Tiamat.

More recently, thanks to the work of Sylvia Perera, Diane Wolkstein, and Betty Meador,[2] I have become intrigued by the cycle of myths associated with the Sumerian goddess Inanna. In these stories sibling experience is focal; they center on Inanna's relation to her sister goddess, Ereshkigal, and to her human sister-in-law, Geshtinanna, on her relation to her brother, the sun god, Utu, and to her mortal brotherly spouse, Dumuzi. The relation between Dumuzi and Geshtinanna, a mortal brother-sister pair, is also important. Though like all such archaic myths, the story can be interpreted with reference to the agricultural cycle and to the rituals of political succession, it self-evidently also speaks profoundly of the human discovery of the painful association of love and death. Because the central figures are female, it speaks particularly to women's experience of yearning and fulfillment, selfishness and love, loss and reconciliation. The myth suggests that sibling experience provides the most adequate metaphors for exploration of these themes.

Sylvia Perera looks upon the story of Inanna's descent to her sister Ereshkigal's underworld realm, the land of no return, as a description of a woman's journey to her own unknown inner depths, a fearful journey that may entail a repulsive decomposition of the way of being in the world with which the woman has until now identified. Perera understands the sisterly relation between the goddesses as signifying that Ereshkigal represents Inanna's neglected, devalued other side. This myth, she suggests, may appeal particularly to women who were so unnurtured by their mothers that the primary Greek myth about a female descent to the underworld has no reassuring power for them. Such women may have difficulties with the Demeter/Persephone myth because they cannot believe in a mother who would mourn their descent or welcome their return.[3]

The psychological meaning Perera finds in the story is persuasive and profound. I believe it reaches to the very heart of the myth—yet when I first read her book I discovered that the Inanna-Ereshkigal encounter also helped me to understand events that happen *between* sisters, between women, and not only *within* them. I was grateful for its illumination of the love that relates me to the woman with whom I live, how it clarified the power of the attraction that binds us and the misunderstandings that persistently appear. I see myself as a woman at home in Inanna's realm, a woman who spends most of her time in the world of relationship, of fertility and joy, but who knows the need of journeys to the underworld for renewal and for reordering. I mean by "underworld" not simply the realm of literal death but that inner place to which we are taken when ongoing life in the everyday world has been brought to a standstill—by an irremediable failure, an unbearable loss, by paralyzing anxiety, or unavoidable guilt. Ordinary life practically ceases and something else begins, subtle and painful but transformative. My lover, especially in earlier years but even now, lives much in the underworld; she is intimately familiar with its every fissure and abyss, but in some ways is less friendly toward it than I— because the other world, the upper world, the world of others and of everyday functioning, often seems painfully inaccessible, almost unreal. We had thought the underworld would be the scene of our deepest meetings; we have found that it is rarely so. *There* we are alone. Thus though I see the Inanna myth as helping me to understand our relationship, I also see it as disclosing once again that journeys to the underworld, soul journeys, are in some inevitable ways solitary journeys.

Ereshkigal, according to Sumerian mythology, is a goddess who goes back to the first days, the very first days. After the sky god carried off the heavens and the air god carried off the earth, she was *given* the underworld as her domain. Indeed, according to some variants, Ereshkigal was herself originally a heavenly goddess who was *taken* to the underworld against her will by Kur, a name that like the Greek Hades refers both to a male underworld deity and to the underworld itself. In either case, the point is that Ereshkigal did not choose this realm, that it is her destiny, as it will be ours. The myth recounts that Enki, the god of wisdom, sets out to rescue her but to no avail; she had entered the land of no return. There she rules as queen—parentless, husbandless, childless, full of rage, greed, and sexual longing, and painfully alone.

Inanna is not literally her sister; she belongs to a much younger generation of gods and goddesses. But as she becomes the most powerful of all upper-world deities, she comes to deserve the sisterly designation. (And in any case "sister" and "brother" are understood less narrowly in this culture than in ours—Inanna calls Gilgamesh, who on our terms is her maternal second cousin, "brother," and she addresses her husband, Dumuzi, in the same way.) To begin with, Inanna is a young maiden, daughter of the moon god and moon goddess, herself associated with the morning and evening star, a maiden who is afraid of the gods of sky and earth and waiting to grow up, waiting for marriage bed and throne. She asks her brother, Utu, god of the sun, for help; he refuses, but Gilgamesh agrees to carve her throne and bed. The myth describes her then, happy with her new possessions and "rejoicing at her wondrous vulva"—but still alone. She visits Enki, the god of wisdom, who welcomes her as an equal. They drink beer together, "more and more beer together." Swaying with drink, Enki toasts Inanna, and gives her the high priesthood, the noble crown, the royal throne, truth, the descent to the underworld, the ascent from the underworld, the art of lovemaking, the kissing of the phallus—and much, much more. With each new gift, Inanna responds, "I take them!" Of course, the next morning when Enki awakes more sober, he regrets his generosity and tries to get these holy powers back, but Inanna refuses and eventually he capitulates. Now Inanna has her throne and a plentitude of divine powers, but her marriage bed is still empty. Her brother persuades her to respond to the courtship of the mortal shepherd Dumuzi. Dumuzi stirs her to an awareness of her own passion—"my vulva is full of eagerness like the young moon." They are wed and make love—fifty times—and then Dumuzi, sated, asks leave to go to the palace. As her consort, he now imagines himself the king.

It is at this point that Inanna determines on her journey to the underworld. Having explored all the other gifts bestowed on her by Enki, perhaps she felt it was now time to discover what was meant by the gift of "descent to the underworld," perhaps the complimentary promise of "ascent from the underworld" made it seem a safe enough adventure. The myth gives no reasons; it only tells us that Inanna "opened her ear" to the Great Below, that she abandoned heaven and earth to descend to the underworld. When asked why she has come, she hesitates before answering that she has come to *witness* the funeral rites of Gugalanna, Ereshkigal's husband—though of course it is her own death that she has come to *experience*. (The text says nothing else about this husband—though Wolkstein suggests he may be a Dumuzi surrogate.) Inanna thinks to protect herself by taking with her all her talismans of divine power and sexual allure, but as she makes her way through the seven gates that lead to her sister's realm, one by one they are taken from her. When she enters Ereshkigal's presence, she is naked and bowed low. The underworld goddess looks upon her with the eye of death, and Inanna is turned into a piece of rotting meat hung from a hook.

Luckily Inanna had told her servant that if she did not return within three days after her descent, the servant should seek help from the gods. But her paternal grandfather, the earth god, and her father, the moon god, both refuse. They see Inanna's descent as hubristic. Not satisfied with the Great Above, she had also craved the Great Below; she should have known *no one* returns from the underworld. But Enki, her maternal grandfather (perhaps repentant of his own role in encouraging Inanna's journey), takes pity on her. He sends two strange creatures down to Ereshkigal's throne room, where they find her moaning as though in childbirth. Inanna's death has somehow initiated a deep crisis in Ereshkigal herself, opened her to *feeling* her own misery. They echo her moans, repeat her cries. Their empathy stirs her gratitude—even in the underworld she is not alone after all—and she agrees to release Inanna. At this point in the myth we see how Inanna's journey has been transformative for *Ereshkigal*, has brought *life* to the realm of death.

For Inanna the journey has, in a sense, only begun—because, of course, she learns one cannot return from the underworld as though nothing has happened. Something—in the language of myth, someone—must stay (or else for Ereshkigal, too, it would be as though it were all but a fantasy). Inanna must choose someone to go to the underworld in her place. She cannot bear that it be her faithful servant or her adored sons; initially it seems easy to decide that it should be Dumuzi, who seems hardly to have missed her, so much as he enjoyed exercising royal power in her absence. Dumuzi succeeds in getting Inanna's brother, Utu, and his own sister to help him evade the Erinyes-like *galla* who have been sent to bring him back to the underworld—but eventually there is no evasion: Dumuzi dies. He was, after all, her *mortal* spouse. Geshtinanna's grief fills the city and awakens Inanna's own. The earthly sister's devotion recalls Inanna back to feeling—for she had become as cold, as locked in self-pity, as ruthless in her death-dealing gaze, as Ereshkigal ever was. Inanna now remembers her love for Dumuzi (and not only her disappointment in him), and she is deeply moved by Geshtinanna's abandonment to grief. It is her human "sister" who helps Inanna assimilate her underworld experience. The myth ends with Inanna's decreeing that Dumuzi need spend only half of each year in the underworld, that Geshtinanna may go there in his place for the other half. So Ereshkigal and Inanna each spend half of the year with Dumuzi, half alone, and Geshtinanna, who loved him most deeply, is separated from him always. (I do wish as I reflect on the ending that they might have been allowed, as the Dioscuri were, to be together in each realm rather than forever apart!)

This Sumerian myth of the meeting between Inanna and Ereshkigal reminds me more of Psyche's encounter with Persephone than of Persephone's own abduction by Hades. The Inanna and Psyche stories both suggest that a woman's soul journey leads her toward engagement with a sisterly figure. I see Inanna as like the Psyche I wanted to imagine, a Psyche who returns to Persephone's realm ready for all that it might require of her. I find the Sumerian tale of Inanna's twofold engagement—with the sister who is goddess of death, who has lived as *lack* all that Inanna herself has lived as power and joy, and with the human sister who understands the inseparability of love and loss—perhaps the most beautiful celebration of the mysteries of sisterhood that I have come to know.

Not that one can really make such a choice. For I think almost immediately of an aspect of Egyptian mythology that has served just as significantly to deepen my appreciation of the full significance of sisterly relationships.

In order to speak adequately of that, I need to begin by considering the one Egyptian myth in which sisterly relationships in the literal sense play an important role, the myth that focuses on the figure of Isis. The Isis tradition is, also, indirectly connected to Psyche, for the Apuleius tale about Cupid and Psyche is (as noted earlier) set within his novella *The Golden Ass,* a fictive account of its protagonist's initiation into the Isis mysteries of the Graco-Roman world. Yet the Isis of this Hellenistic cult is far different from the Isis of early Egyptian mythology. The later Isis has absorbed all the powers and attributes not only of her Egyptian sister goddesses but of the Greek goddesses as well. She is especially closely identified with Aphrodite, as a goddess of love and fertility, and with Demeter, as a goddess of agriculture (and, indeed, of all the civilizing arts, including writing) and as a goddess who protects us from the fearsomeness of death. She is seen as *the* Mother and is most often depicted holding her infant son, Horus, in her lap—these representations become the prototype for early Christian portrayals of the Virgin Mother.[4]

But the Egyptians knew her more as sister than as mother. The version of her myth most accessible to us is provided by Plutarch, and thus it, too, is permeated with a Hellenistic tint—there is, for example, a scene clearly borrowed by the Latin author from *The Homeric Hymn to Demeter* that shows Isis in the role of wet nurse trying to make another woman's child immortal by holding it over a fire—but dynastic reliefs and ritual texts make clear that in its general outlines the tale is authentically Egyptian.

It involves the four children of the sky goddess, Nut, and earth god, Geb—Osiris and Set, Isis and Nepthys, a pair of rival brothers and of deeply bonded sisters. Nut carried them all in her womb at the same time and gave birth to them on succeeding days. Osiris is god of the Nile and ruler of Egypt. Set is god of the desert—in the early traditions simply the necessary polar other to Osiris, in the late period an embodiment of moral evil. Osiris is married to Isis, goddess of the fertile earth that bounds the river; Set to Nepthys, goddess of that strip of land that serves as border between the fertile valley and the sterile desert.

Nepthys, so the story begins, is barren. Longing for children, she entices Osiris to her bed—by getting him drunk or by disguising herself as her sister. In either case, she succeeds; she conceives and bears a child, Anubis, the jackal god of death, of embalming and of funeral rite. Isis, sympathetic with her sister's plight, agrees to raise the child. Set, not too surprisingly, is less complaisant and determines on revenge for the adultery. He invites Osiris to a banquet, where he displays an intricately carved and softly lined coffin and induces Osiris to see for himself how beautifully comfortable it is. As Osiris lowers himself into the coffin, Set quickly closes its lid and sets it floating down the Nile.

When she learns what has happened, Isis sets out in search of her brother-spouse and eventually finds the coffin in the reedy marshes of the far-distant delta. As the bark on which she is bringing her brother-husband's corpse slowly sails back up the river, Isis in her vulture form flutters over his body; her gently flapping wings urge his phallus to rise. She lowers herself onto him and manages to conceive their child, Horus. In time, Set learns of their return and manages to steal Osiris' body, to cut it up into fourteen pieces, and to bury each in a different Egyptian village. Eventually Isis manages to recover all but one of the pieces (the phallus, of course, being the missing part, but she magically fashions a replacement for it) and to re-member Osiris, who then becomes god of the afterworld. When Horus grows up, he successfully challenges Set and assumes the throne of Egypt; Set returns to the desert.

As I have told this story thus far, the emphasis has fallen on Isis' successful struggle against one brother, Set, and her dedicated search for, recovery of, and restoration to life of the other brother, Osiris. The myth obviously again brings together the themes of sisterhood and death—Isis is the sister who restores Osiris not to life on earth but life in the afterworld, life in death. I am also aware that for me this story, so deeply resonant with inner experience, also has relevance to interpersonal experience. I see it as illuminating some of what happened between me and my brother after his wife's sudden and so painfully

early death—which was also a death for him and a dismemberment. As his whole life fell apart, he turned to me after years
of little intimacy to help him gather the pieces back together.

But Isis not only sisters her brother, she is sistered by her
sister, Nepthys, whose loyalty throughout the years of struggle
with Set remains with Isis and not with her spouse. The aid of
Nepthys' magic powers is necessary to restore Osiris' sexual
potency and later to help the infant Horus recover from the
scorpion sting with which Set hopes to kill him. Nepthys is there
to serve as midwife when Horus is born; she accompanies her
sister as they gather Osiris' dismembered body; she helps fash-
ion the surrogate phallus; her son, Anubis, helps the two sisters
embalm the re-membered god. Indeed, there is much to suggest
that early on Isis and Nepthys were viewed as almost equally
powerful goddesses. The two sisters appear facing one another—equally powerful, equally beautiful—in many reliefs,
frescoes, papyri. They stand supporting a scarab between them
or kneel in worshipful posture before a mummiform Osiris;
one guards the head, the other the foot, of a dead man ready
to begin his journey to the afterworld. Along with Neith and
Selket, they are shown protecting the canopic jars that held the
deceased's entrails and guard the outer coffin.

Plutarch's myth about Isis and Osiris and Isis and Nepthys
originated in the early pharaonic period and served a political
function in stabilizing and validating the transition from one
ruler's reign to the next. The hieroglyph that identifies Isis is a
throne; in reliefs and sculptures she is often shown wearing a
throne on her head. The implication is clear: Isis represents the
divine power of the ancient goddesses upon which the authority
of the kings and even the male gods in some sense continues to
rest. (The reliefs at Abydos that show the goddess protectively
enclosing Seti I within her wings give beautiful testimony to
this.) Plutarch's version—though it acknowledges that these gods
and goddesses are related to aspects of the natural world—
presents them as though they were as fully humanlike as the
Greek divinities with whom he was more familiar. His representation makes the myth more available to psychological interpretation—but fails to do justice to the uniqueness of Egyptian
mythological consciousness.

The throne symbol may, in fact, be delusive, misleading; for

Isis, like all the Egyptian divinities, is primarily not a political but a nature goddess, a descendant of the prehistoric vulture goddess who was associated with both birth and death. Throughout all periods of Egyptian history she was often represented with a vulture headdress and with the vulture's widespreading wings. Human-shaped divinities appear in Egypt along with the first pharaohs but in Egypt do not as elsewhere replace the earlier theriomorphic representations. Indeed, the animal forms, the mixed hybrid forms (usually human body with animal head), and the human forms were all seen as equally valid expressions of the divine beings. In Egypt the recognition of the sacredness of the natural world, including its animal inhabitants, was not characteristic only of some early, later discarded, animistic phase, but persisted long after the introduction of anthropomorphic deities. Even in its most mature phase Egyptian religion still communicated a recognition of the divinity, the transcendence, of the natural world. Their relationship to nature was in no way sentimental; the animals they worshiped were often fearful and destructive—like the lion and the hippopotamus, the crocodile and the scorpion.

The Egyptian understanding of death was closely allied to this sense of their interdependence with the natural world. The deceased were buried on the western side of the Nile so that they might there enter the underworld as the sun does each evening. Egyptians hoped in death to become Osiris—what this means may be best communicated by recalling the most common image of the underworld god, which shows him wrapped like a human mummy with grain stalks growing from his body. They hoped also to rise from the underworld like the sun and move into the heavens where they would join the stars.[5]

What, you might ask, does this have to do with *sisters?* To my mind—everything. For from Egyptian mythology I have begun to learn that the other creatures with whom we humans share this planet are our sisters and brothers—as the ants who helped Psyche are her sisters (not just symbols of a sisterly aspect of herself). Every day the vultures circle the canyon at whose edge I live. I recognize Isis as they wheel past, as truly as I recognize her in Plutarch's tale. Egyptian mythology has opened me to a new dimension of the ever-reappearing connection between

sisterhood and death—to a realization that our failure to recognize our sisterhood with all that lives may lead to the end of
life here on this planet. Will we, we human women and men,
learn to live with these other forms of life as our siblings or will
our insistence on our own uniqueness, on our privileged right
to have dominion over every other living creature, lead us to
destroy them and ourselves?

It is strange in a way how these myths of five thousand years
ago, the myths of Sumer and Egypt that antedate Homer and
Genesis by two millennia, present an understanding of what
sisterly experience most deeply means that lies *beyond* what I
already knew. What these myths call upon us to recognize seems
not at all a nostalgic pull back to some regressive, pre-Oedipal
blissful experience of fusion. They do not summon us back to
an escapist fantasy of the recreation of a mother goddess-dominated world; they summon us *forward*—to a new understanding
of what sisterhood *might mean.*

Such a new understanding seems, however, to depend on our
understanding first, clearly and honestly, what it *has* meant in
the traditions that have most shaped Western consciousness and
what it *does* mean in the less conscious strata of our own psyches.
The Greek myths were relevant to this urgent prior task, as are
also the traditions about sibling experience we have inherited
from Israel, whose influence on our culture is almost equally
powerful. I see the divine sisters of Sumerian and Egyptian
mythology supplementing, expanding, transforming our understanding of sisterhood. They help us to reimagine its meaning.
The other major culture of the ancient near eastern world,
Israel, gives us something different, but its offering is also one
we cannot afford to ignore. For the Bible's assumptions live in
us just as deeply as do those communicated by Greek tragedy.
When we turn to the Bible—and in this context I mean by that
primarily a turn to the legends of Genesis—we find ourselves
again in a world where brotherhood is seen almost entirely in
human terms, and where sisterhood is almost entirely ignored.

Among the Hebrews even more than among the Greeks the
focus falls on *male* experience. The underlying matrifocal world

whose subordination plays such a central role in other mythologies is so deeply obscured in this tradition as to be—almost—eliminated. We discern its hidden presence in the tale about Adam and Eve in which, uniquely, the female plays the central role. The text even acknowledges that her name means "Mother of All That Lives," that it derives from the verb *to be* just as the name YHVH does; modern etymology suggests Eve's name may connect her to the Mesopotamian dragon/snake/serpent goddess, the ancient mother of all. We know that in other traditions the serpent who is here viewed as an agent of evil is associated with fertility, immortality, and wisdom. It is not hard to see in this story where woman is born of man an attempt to deny man's dependence on woman—to see it as a story where the primordial goddess is transformed into the subordinated human female, where the goddess who is source of life and death, blessing and suffering, becomes the woman who is responsible for the evils in human life. (The folktale about Adam's *first* wife, Lilith, whom he rejected because she insisted on their equality—even in bed!—confirms how central to this story is the insistence on Adam's privileged position vis-à-vis Eve.) Yet the story's testimony is more ambiguous than may at first appear—as Milton recognized when he wrote of the "fortunate" fall. Was Eve's greater curiosity, her willingness to break the divine taboo (and isn't the point in every tale about taboos the violation?), really all loss?[6]

It is her deed that brings us into this world of struggle and confusion in which we still live. But after this first story, the actors are almost all men. The only *named* children of Adam and Eve are their three sons: Cain and Abel and Seth. As the Genesis account unfolds, the struggle between brothers, from Cain and Abel to Joseph and his many brothers, is what shapes human being, a struggle passed down from generation to generation, shape-shifting yet ever recurring.

This is obvious in the biblical text itself, but my appreciation of the significance of the brother theme in this tradition has been immeasurably deepened by Thomas Mann's retelling of the tales in *Joseph and His Brothers*.[7] I am impressed, too, by how Mann's understanding of the Genesis stories is enriched by his awareness of his intensely ambivalent relationship to his own brother, Heinrich, and how, in turn, his own experience must have been illuminated by his exploration of the biblical paradigms.

Mann's sense of how history and myth co-create each other becomes a theme in the novel itself, a theme announced in its first pages: "Very deep is the well of the past . . . " So many of the figures in his story are themselves aware of reliving what has been lived before—albeit differently. Jacob's servant, Eliezer, is, and is not, the same Eliezer who served Abraham; there has always been an Eliezer. As Jacob retells his family's legends he forgets what he witnessed, what he knows only through having been told it long ago. Joseph understands as he lies at the bottom of the well into which his brothers have thrown him that he is "repeating" a mythical pattern, that in some sense he "is" Adonis, Tammuz, Ganymede, Christ. In his essay "Freud and the Future," Mann writes more explicitly of his sense of how our lives are enriched when we come to recognize in them this strange intermingling of the unique and the typical, the individual and the mythical. When this mythical point of view becomes conscious, we are, he says, granted "a smiling knowledge of the eternal."[8] Mann's retelling thus explicitly invites us to recognize ourselves in the ancient tales.

History begins with the two brothers Cain and Abel and with Cain's murder of Abel, whom God preferred. Mann helps us see that from the biblical perspective this is how it has to begin. There could not be only one brother—we humans are created for relationship not solitude. Two brothers as close to one another, as alike, as two humans can be, and yet *other*—that in itself is somehow unbearable; we should be exactly the same, or there should be only one. The murder expresses that; but it cannot change the basic situation. Abel is gone; but then there is Seth. That there are two means there is *life,* means there will be misunderstanding, betrayal, suffering—and sometimes reconciliation. Mann—offering us a "feast of storytelling"—tries to help us see that God created the world because he loves stories, loves the concrete and particular not the abstract.

Though Cain and Abel provide the dark background, Mann's retelling really begins with Abraham. Again there are two sons, Ishmael and Isaac. Again, preference is given to the younger. The older is not killed but banished—the blessing will be given to the "true wife's" child. The decision is Sarah's; the deed is Abraham's, and it is he who must then suffer the test of being asked to sacrifice the other son as well. Ishmael is banished, so one story has it, for "sporting" with Isaac. Was the problem, this time, that the brothers were too *close?* That they needed to *be* separated?

Isaac in turn has two sons, Esau and Jacob. Mann is at his best as he shows how deeply Isaac loves both his sons, how he couldn't bear to send Esau away as his father had sent Ishmael away. And yet the blessing cannot be divided, and he has to choose himself, that is, the youngest son. He is aware of having to live again what has already been lived, but he does so in protest—that is, he allows himself to be tricked into giving the blessing to Jacob, the younger son. Blind, he doesn't have to see what he does—though he cannot, after all, avoid the painful confrontation with his betrayed older son. (Again, it seems worth noting, the mother is more determined in this matter of which son should receive the blessing.)

Ishmael pretty much disappears from the story once he has been sent away. Esau does not. Beautifully, poignantly proud, at that moment when he enters his father's tent expectant, Esau accepts his disappointment, his destined role, with dignity. Mann presents him as consciously refusing to fulfill the Cain role— and as coming to meet Jacob after their long years of separation in full forgiveness, a forgiveness that the trickster brother has difficulty in crediting.

During Jacob's years in the household of his mother's brother, Laban, he comes to marry two sisters, the daughters of his host. In *Genesis,* a book so full of tales of brotherhood, these two, Leah and Rachel, are the only sisters to appear. From the moment of his arrival Jacob falls in love with the younger, Rachel, and for seven years dreams toward their wedding night. As Mann tells the story, Rachel knows all along that he will be given Leah first; it is after all the custom in their world that the oldest must be the first to wed and that many a man will have more than one wife. The two sisters, deeply bonded, weep together on the eve of the wedding—Rachel because she must wait and Jacob will feel betrayed, Leah because she knows she is not really wanted. In the darkness of the bridal chamber Jacob uses his hands to see—as Isaac had when giving the blessing—and makes love to his bride with all the full and innocent passion of a virgin groom. Later he realizes that this first night's lovemaking cannot be taken back any more than could Isaac's gift. Laban soon gives Jacob Rachel as well, and clearly she is the wife he *loves*. In recompense God opens Leah's womb and keeps Rachel's closed. Of course, each sister comes to envy the other: Leah longs to have Jacob come to her with desire; Rachel longs to bear children. When Rachel finally gives birth to Joseph, Leah has to watch her own six sons displaced by her sister's one. The one tale of sisterhood serves primarily to demonstrate how tragically sisters are set against one another in a world of fathers and brothers.

Jacob, as we have noted, in his turn has sons, twelve sons, and a favorite among them, Joseph, not the very youngest but nearly so, the first child of the "true wife," Rachel. (Her second child, Benjamin, brought her death and so would always be for Jacob too painfully associated with that death to win the spontaneously free-flowing devotion he felt for Joseph.) Jacob's favoritism is blatantly displayed—and aggravated by Joseph's naive, narcissistic self-delight. Of course, the other brothers covet the love that only Joseph receives; of course, they realize the hopelessness of their situation: the only way to win that love would be by killing Joseph, yet the deed itself would mean the forfeit of the hoped-for gain. Mann gives us a vivid sense of the individual character of each of Leah's ten sons, especially of the eldest, Reuben, who truly loves Joseph *and* resents his privileged position, who is determined *not* to be Cain and yet cannot avoid participating in the deeds that lead to Joseph's being taken to Egypt. When Jacob learns of Joseph's supposed death, he is as overtaken by grief as was Demeter when she lost Persephone. He rails at God, admits he could not pass the test laid on Abraham when called upon to sacrifice Isaac—yet gradually as the years pass (albeit never explicitly), he acknowledges his complicity. Somehow he and Joseph's brothers learn to live together in penance and in guilt.

Joseph was the favored one—yet also the one destined to recapitulate the exile of the disfavored brother, of Cain, Ham, and Ishmael. But this time around there is *content* to that exile, the self-absorbed youth who was thrown into the well "dies" and over the years becomes someone who can see how things look from the other side, not just from his own. That, in these biblical tales, seems to be the *point* of brotherly experience—the real discovery, acceptance, and blessing of the otherness of a beloved other. The change begins while he is in the well. For the first time he realizes how he has provoked his brothers and feels guilt for the grief soon to overwhelm his father. But it takes all the many adventures that Joseph lives through while he is in Egypt to fully effect the change.

And so as this long sequence of tales about brotherly struggle comes to its end, there can be a reconciliation. The brothers come to Egypt, and Joseph introduces himself to them; their refusal to allow Benjamin to be kept behind as token of their return while they go back for Jacob convinces Joseph that they, too, have changed during the intervening years. At the end of the story, when it comes time for Jacob to give his deathbed blessing, it goes to Judah not Joseph; Jacob asks to be buried with Leah not Rachel; things cannot always go according to feeling. The brothers meet again after Jacob's burial, still a little fearful that with their father dead Joseph's apparent forgiveness may turn out to be a mirage. Joseph reassures them:

When you talk to me of forgiveness it seems to me you have missed the meaning of the whole story we are in. I do not blame you for that. One can easily be in a story and not understand it. . . . But if it is a question of pardon between us human beings, then it is I myself who must beg for it, for you had perforce to be cast in the villain's part so that things might turn out as they did.[9]

"So endeth," Mann tells us, "the beautiful story and God-invention of Joseph and His Brothers." So endeth, also, my examination of the myths and folktales that have shaped our culture's imaginings about sibling experience. It remains now to look at how this dimension of human experience has been reimagined in our time by what I take to be *our* mythologists, our tellers of tales about the psyche—the depth psychologists.

II
PSYCHOLOGY'S SISTERS

You are every woman I ever loved
and disavowed

—Adrienne Rich

7. ReSearching Siblings

Having looked carefully at the testimony of mythology about sibling experience, and in particular at its representations of sisterly interactions, I want now to explore how the sister bond has been envisioned in more recent times—particularly by psychology, for I see psychology as providing us with the *logos* of the *psyche*, the speech about the soul, that speaks most powerfully to us. Thus fully to understand our souls' apprehension of what sisterhood means requires attending to what Adler and Jung and Freud have to say and then examining how feminists have responded to their articulations.

When I first turned my attention to what the three "fathers" of depth psychology might contribute to our understanding of sister-sister relationships I quickly discovered that I was not alone in my long neglect of this kinship bond. None of them ever really focused on the meaning of a woman's relationship to her sisters in their psychology of women. All three offer interesting observations about the hostility between brothers and its transformation into devotion and about the mythological motif of brother-sister incest but have almost nothing to say about the bond between sisters. It is as though the significance of that bond is even more hidden from the sons and brothers whose *theoria*, whose visions, created depth psychology than is the mother-daughter bond. The relationship appears to be even more invisible to these modern men than it was to the men of fifth-century Athens. Despite this, depth psychology does "deepen" our understanding, partly by showing *why* the relationship is so invisible, partly by its more general interpretations of the heavily charged lifelong significance of primary relationships.

Psychoanalytical theory was, as we all know, in large measure created from a male perspective and from the perspective of patriarchal culture. In patriarchy stress is traditionally laid on contrasexual relationships and on heterosexuality, on the spousal bond and on the nuclear triangular family: mother, father, son. Sex means power, possession, and inheritance. But in matrilineal societies (and remember, still today, all of us begin our lives in a matrifocal environment) for both women and men clan loyalty is more important than marital loyalty and the blood ties to parents and siblings take precedence over the relationships with spouses or offspring. (Remember the importance of the struggle between these two conceptions in Greek mythology and tragedy.) Perhaps it is not surprising that male theory has minimized the significance of sibling experience in general, and same-sex sibling interaction in particular, and has almost entirely ignored sister-sister relationships—even though in the mother tongue of depth psychology, German, the word for sibling, *Geschwister,* is an intensification of the word for sister, *Schwester.*

Of the three founders of depth psychology, Adler, whose claim to be a *depth* psychologist is somewhat suspect, is the one in whose thinking siblings most explicitly play a central role. Yet, although he validates the intrinsic significance of sibling relationships, he confines his focus to the interactions that occur in childhood and ignores the role gender might play in these interactions. Jung, who writes almost entirely of adult experience, lays stress on just those symbolic inner dimensions that Adler ignores but is primarily interested in how the inner relationship to the *contra-sexual* sibling helps free us from a mother-dominated psychology. Freud offers us a rich interpretation of the interplay between childhood and adulthood, between inner and outer, but has little to say about the female experience of sibling interaction. I have learned from each, but my hope that my own intuitions about the particular meaning that sisterly relationship has for women might be directly addressed has not been met—nor, as we'll see, is it fully met by the feminist revisionings of psychology.

I will begin by looking at Adler's contributions because sibling experience has greater salience in his theory than in that of Freud or Jung. Although I knew before beginning this study that Adler had brought sibling interaction into the forefront of psychological theory out of the obscurity to which he felt it consigned by Freud, my prejudices about Adlerian theory had led me to expect he would have little to say about sibling experience as a mystery in the deeper sense invoked at the end of my Introduction. Now as I reconsider the full import of Adler's conviction that a logos of the psyche that so fetishizes the relationship between parent and child as to overlook the intrinsic significance of the relationship among siblings will radically misunderstand how we become who we are, I wonder whether my earlier somewhat supercilious dismissal of Adler may not have been an artifact of my neglect of the importance of my sister in my own life—and perhaps of my uncritical assumption of the perspectives of an eldest child.

For Adler's personality theory is, as he was the first to acknowledge, constructed from the perspective of a second child. His discovery of the significance of sibling birth order, one of the most widely acclaimed aspects of his theory, arose out of his struggle to understand the source of his differences from Freud (as Jung's theory of psychological types was created out of his desire to understand what underlies the differences of theoretical vision among Freud, Adler, and himself). Adler sees the early-established patterns determined by one's birth order as continuing into adulthood, as central to our way of being in the world.

Adler came to see Freud's psychology as representative of the psychology of the first, the pampered child. He believes that Freud's focus on the Oedipus complex and on the child's intensely ambivalent relation to its parents derive from his having been an eldest child and thus having a natural tendency to overemphasize the importance of the mother-child relationship. As a second child, Adler believes himself to be just as naturally more aware of the importance and complexity of sibling interaction. Freud's seeing in the sibling only a rival for parental affection, Adler regards as peculiar to a first child's perspective. Because initially an "only," the first child will experience "dethronement" upon the birth of another sibling more traumatically than any later born child. The intense and ruthless hostility, the murderous impulses, that Freud considers to be universally present between siblings, Adler dismisses as the self-indulgent exaggeration typical of the eldest child.

Much that is most characteristic of Freud's psychology—the prediliction for antithetical thinking (especially the insistence on the discontinuity between consciousness and the unconscious), the romantic exaggeration of the importance of sexuality, the therapeutic pessimism, the emphasis on intrapsychic rather than interpersonal dynamics, the focus on the infantile past rather than the adult present, the conviction that insight not cure or happiness is the appropriate goal of therapy, and, above all, the "poetic license," the mythologizing—Adler attributes to a first child's typical, but neurotic, nostalgia for the never recoverable time when all his parents' devotion devolved upon him.[1]

The second-born, who must from the beginning share parental attention, has (so Adler believes) a different view of everything. When the firstborn typically dreams of falling, the second will dream of running after trains or failing to catch up in a race. Indeed, each subsequent sibling has a unique perspective. Youngest children, for example, have no followers but many pacemakers; challenged in many directions, they often develop in an extraordinary way. No wonder, Adler observes, that "in every fairy tale the youngest child surpasses all his brothers and sisters." Adler believes that even when there is no actual sibling, a child lives as though there were. An only child may direct a feeling of competition against the father and thus make of the father a sibling surrogate.[2]

Adler's own psychological theory represents the perspective of a second child who, because never subject to the radical dethronement the first experiences, sees everything in less dramatic terms. Thus Adler in contrast to Freud sees continuity between the concerns of waking and dream life; his vision is pragmatic and concrete where Freud's is theoretical and symbolic. Adler is more present-focused and more optimistic about the possibility of cure. Whereas the first child typically knows only competition, the second is, he says, "a little closer to cooperation."

Adler's vision of the most important task in human life—the development of what he calls "fellow feeling"—is an extrapolation into the wider social sphere of sibling interdependence. He believes that the real issue in therapy is always undeveloped social interest and that tendency to think in terms of antithetical polarities which leads one to see every situation in terms of dominance or submission, superiority or inferiority, rather than in terms of cooperation. Maturity comes from the recognition that "inferiority" really means interdependence.[3]

In Adler's view all of us as children experience ourselves as inferior; to compensate many of us try to establish ourselves as superior. The will to power is the omnipresent motivation, to Adler self-evidently more important than sexual desire. But first children who find themselves in relation only to the overwhelmingly superior power of their parents may need to shield themselves from recognizing the full significance of a struggle for power they have no chance of winning. Because second children have from the beginning the experience of a relationship with a relatively equal peer, the discovery that neither dependence nor independence but rather interdependence is the real truth of human involvement may come more easily to them.

For Adler neurosis is an expression of the failure to recognize the inner meaning of sibling experience; the neurotic is trapped in the fantasy of being the only child, in the illusion of isolation. Since therapy is training in cooperation, the therapist's most important work is modeling fellow feeling, demonstrating the ability to experience the fellow human–ness of the patient. What the psyche, the soul, most deeply wants is community— learning how to relate to others free of the ego's fearful obsession with the polarities of dominance and submission.[4]

As I reread Adler, I have come to appreciate that he is more of a "depth" psychologist than I had earlier recognized when taking him to be speaking only of the literal bond between biological siblings. Actually, like Freud, his observations are based on retrospective recollection and are directed toward helping us understand how our attitudes in the present are shaped by our remembered versions of our earliest experiences. I also celebrate his recognition of the intrinsic meaning of sibling interaction and its lifelong influence, as well as his sense that the most adequate model of mature human relationships is based on sibling interdependence. Yet although Adler confirms my intuition that sibling interaction is not only an important part of childhood experience but also something that shapes us throughout our lives, he never looks at how the relation between siblings continues and changes through the life span; he considers only what happens in childhood and its continuing effects.

Adler also disappoints because he has nothing to say relevant to my conviction that sister-sister bonding is intrinsically different from sister-brother or even brother-brother bonding. In his discussion of birth order and sibling interaction Adler makes no specific reference to gender. He makes no distinction between the interrelationships of same-sex and contra-sex siblings nor between the perspectives of an oldest sister and an oldest brother.

(Elsewhere, despite his belief that our culture's denigration of the feminine promotes a hypermasculinity in its men and a consequent overvaluation of the striving for power, Adler clearly accepts rather conventional understandings of what constitutes appropriate masculinity and femininity. He often identifies maturity with the acceptance of one's gender as an unchangeable given.)

Almost in passing, Adler does remark that an only boy with many sisters (or an only girl with many brothers) is likely to develop exaggeratedly masculine (or feminine) qualities. In these situations gender identification feels tenuous and threatened. There are no other references to gender in Adler's discussion of sibling experience. (Even the gender of the parents is much less important from his perspective than from Freud's; a child will prefer whichever parent pampers him the most, irrespective of what Oedipal theory might predict.)

Adler's lack of emphasis on gender may reflect his conviction that elder-younger is a more fundamental issue than male-female and his desire to demystify Freud's tendency to sexualize all human encounter. Nevertheless it appears expressive of the common assumption that male experience is paradigmatic of human experience, an assumption evident in the ease with which Adler speaks of the child always as "he," as I have done in discussing his theory. Although I may learn from Adler about those aspects of my experience that are generically human, I receive no illumination of those that are specifically female.

What I most value is his conviction that the overcoming of the limitations of perspective correlative with a particular birth order is one of our most important soul tasks. I do, indeed, understand that so long as I respond to the world only as an oldest child, as an elder sister, I am stuck. Adler has helped me understand that there is an inner younger sister potential within me whose quite different perspective I must make my own.

Yet—perhaps because I *am* an oldest child—Adler continues to disappoint me. I hunger for a different kind of "depth," for a more mythologically informed perspective—for more recognition of the great variety of human patterns of experience, more recognition of the persistence of ambiguity and ambivalence, more awareness that although interdependence may be a valid ideal in reality most of us continue to also want to be fully independent and entirely dependent. After reading the myths, Adler's often seems a fairy-tale view.

Despite Adler's innovative and imaginative exploration of the sibling bond, this dimension of human experience received almost no attention from other psychologists for many decades. Adler has always been the ignored depth psychologist, and for a long while his emphasis on siblings was ignored as well.

Until recently—for quite suddenly psychology has in the last ten years or so rediscovered sisters and brothers.[5] My own sense of it being time to give attention to the meaning of sisterhood seemed to be intrinsically determined by the rhythms of my own life. Yet once again (as when I discovered how much my dream-inspired search for the hidden goddess was one many other women were already engaged in) I find that an almost entirely neglected area of study—the significance of sibling relationships—is at present being given more attention, at least among psychologists. My neglect, my rediscovery, seem to be correlative with a cultural shift of consciousness.

There are elements of our current social circumstances that may help explain why the significance of this particular familial relationship should suddenly again become more visible—although admitting to them does not entirely dissolve my sense of a mysterious synchronicity. Several fairly recent changes to the pattern of family life dominant in the middle-class West since about 1850 (dominant, that is, in the world in which the "fathers" of psychological and sociological theory grew up) appear relevant. With more mothers working, with more marriages disrupted by divorce, children may more consciously and obviously be turning to one another for primary emotional support. (Research confirms that sibling attachments are greater when parents are unavailable—literally or experientially absent, weak, or dead.) Smaller families, fewer siblings, may heighten the intensity of the connections that do exist and stimulate more awareness of their importance. Thus for contemporary children the interrelationships among siblings may be of greater significance than they were for their parents as children.

But also for the parents as adults—for us—siblings may now be of more evident importance than they were at earlier periods in our lives. Our own divorces may lead us to discover that our original blood ties are after all more primary than the marital bond. As more of us live longer, we may find ourselves outliving spouses but finding that siblings (who share the genetic heritage that in part determines life span) are still alive. (Empirical studies suggest that the proportion of the population with a living sibling remains remarkably constant throughout adulthood: over 80 percent.)[6] When parents die, siblings often come to represent the family of origin. As more of us live longer, we may also find ourselves engaging in that "regressive" return to origins, to the originally primary connections and feelings, that Freud thought to characterize old age.

The greater interest in sibling relationships on the part of psychologists may be reflective not only of there being more to see but also of changes in how psychologists look. The more general acceptance within psychology of the importance of the entire life span, including the middle and later years (in contrast to an earlier focus on childhood and adolescence) makes it easier to recognize the lifelong importance of sibling relationships. Psychological interest in siblings has, no doubt, also been encouraged by the increasing popularity of family systems theory, which focuses on complex reciprocal relationships within families rather than (as traditionally) on the single, isolated "identified patient."

As the shape and significance of sibling interactions in our own culture change, it may help us to be more aware of the diversity of ways in which these relationships have been lived in other times and places. In most cultures the sibling relationship remains an intact, indeed a central, bond throughout the life span.[7] Siblings experience one another as part of a mutually interdependent system that begins in early childhood, when much of the infant caretaking is in the hands of older siblings, and continues into adulthood. Often the sibling relationship takes precedence over the marital bond. In many matrilineal tribes, for example, a man has more responsibility for his sister's children than for his own. Unlike our culture where the relationship between same-sex siblings provides us with an almost unique model of acceptable homo-sexual intimacy, in many human societies it is taken for granted that the most intimate human bonds will be with same-sex others. Our longing to extend the privileges freely granted sisters in our world to other relationships among women implies a widening of the meaning of sisterhood for which there is ample precedent elsewhere.

For the relationship between siblings is not simply a biological given; it is always culturally defined. Many languages don't even have a word for what we call a "sibling" or even for what we mean by "brother" or "sister." The gender of the speaker or the speaker's relative age may determine what word to use. Or there may be no word to distinguish between what we would call a sibling from what we would call a maternal cousin. To extend the sibling bond metanomically to relatives who are not literally born of the same womb, to extend it metaphorically to include nonrelated intimate others, are human practices that long antecede depth psychology. Yet the depth psychologists (as we will see more clearly when we turn to Freud and Jung) help us to understand the role such extensions play in our own psyches.

Although the contemporary researchers recognize their indebtedness to Adler's work, they seem to ignore most of those features of his work that I find most interesting. Their focus is almost entirely on the literal bond between actual siblings and on the external, objective features of their interaction. How different from Adler, who was retrospectively trying to understand the formative power of his own childhood experience! Much of the recent work has consisted primarily of reports on behaviorally oriented research; some, more clinically and phenomenologically oriented, has sought to describe the lifelong meaning of sibling relationships as siblings themselves articulate it.

The research provides some fascinating information about the effects of age differences and gender difference on sibling interaction. Of course, I tend to read it much as I read astrology—in this instance looking not for what I might learn about being a Pisces but for what the research says about what firstborn daughters tend to be like and how they relate to their younger brothers and sisters. Amidst the plethora of tables and statistics, what I notice seems mostly to be what confirms my own experience—or what puzzles. I am helped to remember interactions with my own siblings or interactions among my children. I look for indications of how being older sister to a brother is different from being the older sister of a sister. I nod in agreement and dismay when I am told that being a big sister is a role I carry throughout life. I am especially attentive to studies that reinforce my conviction that the relations among siblings have intrinsic significance, that they cannot be adequately understood simply as determined by rivalry for parental love.

The research informs me that firstborn females like myself tend to be adult-centered even after the arrival of the laterborn children, close to their fathers and very ambivalent in their relation to their mothers. They are likely to be relatively more "masculine" than laterborn females in the same family though less aggressive. We tend, I am told, to be more introverted, more verbal, more critical, more demanding of ourselves. We are curious, original, ambitious, competitive. We have strong superegos and see ourselves as the responsible one. In easy situations, we are conformists but in the more difficult, more important ones, nonconformist. We are often deviant with respect to sex roles. We tend to end up as the dominant partner in our marriages. I weigh this, see how some of it fits, wonder how I would have been different had I not been a first child, wonder what it would be like *now* to enter, at least imaginatively, into the role of a younger sister.[8]

I find the research on the role of "de-identification" in sibling interaction especially interesting.[9] (The term refers to the process whereby siblings separate from one another by claiming different attributes.) I find myself nodding at the findings that emphasize that this process is more likely to occur between same-sex than opposite-sex siblings, that we "tend to compare ourselves with similar others to obtain accurate and stable self-evaluation information." When I read that the process includes "split-parent identification"—which means that in order to defuse rivalry one daughter identifies with the father, the other with the mother—I respond, "But we were both father's daughters; I was like him, and she was his pet." But I agree when I read of how the process involves an exaggeration of perceived rather than objective differences. I smile as I acknowledge how unlikely it would be for anyone to guess from my sister's and my version of our mental and physical attributes how nearly identical are our IQ's, how often even close acquaintances have taken us for each other.

I am also intrigued by the finding that just being different isn't enough: the process of ego differentiation seems to require *polarization*. I well remember believing, "I'm the bright one, and she's the pretty one" but had forgotten how often I'd also felt "I'm fast, she's slow"; "I'm introverted, she's extroverted"; "I'm unconventional, she's conventional"; "I'm achieving, she's nonachieving." Yes, I admit, I thought like that; she probably did, too; and our lists, though probably not identical, probably were much alike. I *still* think like that sometimes, but though it may have been appropriate *then*, surely it isn't now? Not only are we so much more alike than such a schema can encompass, but *I'm* more complex: I'm an achiever *and* a nonachiever, conventional and unconventional, courageous and cowardly, bright and sometimes painfully dumb. I notice, too, that although the literature ha a lot to say about how sisters help one another differentiate, it never asks whether we might at a later point help one another integrate those attributes initially given over to the other.

The research indicates that we tend to try to replicate our family constellation in our adult friendships, that marriages are most successful when there is such replication—when a woman with a younger brother marries a man with an older sister.[10] I recall, that's what my brother did. I acknowledge also that I, a woman with a younger sister, am now involved with a woman who is a second daughter, and I think, but that's our *problem*. Yes, it makes it easier in a way: we so readily fall into a familiar pattern of command and deference or struggle, but surely that familiar pattern is not what we *want!*

Obviously, these recent studies leave me dissatisfied. Their primary emphasis is still on childhood sibling interaction. They seem to be directed more toward advising parents than toward furthering self-understanding. They convey almost nothing of the experiential lived dimension of sibling interaction. Rather than describe what happens between a firstborn child and his or her next-born sibling within a given family, they report only what distinguishes the cohort of first children from the cohort of second children. When researchers are interested in studying how sibling relationships change during the course of the life span, they compare a group of siblings who are now in their fifties with another group now in their twenties. We are given no sense of what really happens to a particular pair of siblings as they interact throughout their lives.

Although the subject is siblings, the assumption often still seems to be that the relation between parent and child is primary and that rivalry for parental attention is the key dimension of sibling interaction. Rarely is John Bowlby's[11] warning not to attach abstract labels to emotions, to pay close attention instead to concrete situations, particular responses, heeded. Don't label it "jealousy," he advises, note what is actually being said or done. Yet the few studies that have actually focused on what happens among siblings when their parents are absent find a great range of emotional connection—less conflict and aggression than when parents are present, much mutual and mutually enjoyed imitation, subtle, esoteric interchanges, empathic understanding of one another's feelings, acceptance of one another's need for help and protection, an ability to provide comfort, above all, a readiness to take into account the other's situation—long before this becomes visible in relationships with adults. These studies confirm how intrinsically important sibling interactions are, that it is here that we often first experience ourselves as separate from yet intimately connected to another who is much like us and yet also different.[12]

Another limitation of most of the empirical studies is that they tend to focus on the search for norms—to look either for statistical averages or for ideal patterns. Such an approach inevitably minimizes the significance of the variety of relationship patterns that actually exist and thus ignores what the myths made so evident—that there are as many different ways of being a sister, even of being an eldest sister, as there are of being a mother, and that no one of them is the "right" way.

Because behavioral research rarely acknowledges the reality of unconscious factors, it is likely to miss precisely what was so central in the mythological perspective: the recognition of the ambivalence inherent in all primary relationships, the *coexistence* of hatred and love, of loyalty and rivalry. These psychological studies also communicate a negative valuation of what are seen as "pathological" patterns. Again, there is little recognition of what the myths highlight—how conflict, struggle, misunderstanding, abandonment, failure are an inescapable dimension of every human life, of every significant relationship, and how much of the richness of our lives is garnered from such "negative" experiences. The research inspired by Adler's pioneering work fails to render sibling experience in a way that gives us a sense of how it is *experienced*—or of how it is passed down from generation to generation.

Of course, what is ignored or denied by the research are just those aspects of sibling relationships that we, too, would often just as soon forget. Freud may have relieved us of feeling shame with respect to infantile sibling rivalry, but it remains difficult to acknowledge that it persists into adulthood. Yet how often as adults in moments of intense interaction with a sibling we discover that the old patterns of competition and abnegation, of dominance and submission, reappear—seemingly out of nowhere. Or how often we discover that an assumed "closeness" dissolves—that an apparently beloved sibling is in actuality the last person with whom we would discuss *this* intimate difficulty or *this* life-shaping decision.

Whereas in almost every other time and place siblings have been forced into lifelong face-to-face interdependence, our culture allows us to believe that we have the freedom to escape the sibling bond, to leave it behind, as though the relationship had ended with our childhood. Yet often a family crisis—the marriage or divorce of a sibling, the illness or death of a parent or spouse, of a child or of another sibling, some serious financial disaster, a long-distance move, the need to share the care of aging parents, or even our dreams—will reveal the persistence of the intensely ambivalent aboriginal feelings. The bond seems to be there "in" us, whether we like it or not. Perhaps that is simply another way of saying that the bond between siblings, between sisters, is archetypal.

This is just what the research literature misses: the archetypal dimension of sibling relationships, and in particular of same-sex sibling relationships. There is little recognition of the role such relationships play in our lives irrespective of literal experience, little sense of the persistence of the intensely ambivalent aboriginal feelings, still so easily aroused in moments of intense adult interaction, still so often spilling over into our later intimate relationships. The symbolic and the inner significance are overlooked.

Yet although the research fails to honor the deeper mysteries of sibling experience, to know what has been learned of sibling interaction in its most empirical and concrete sense helps keep us honest as we seek to understand what "sisterhood" might mean in a more extended sense. These studies also help us see how our experience fits in with that of others. They help us remember what we've forgotten, confront what we've denied, and see more clearly what we long for and need that is not given here. They lead us to long for a *depth* psychology.

8. Inner Sisters

Carl Jung focuses on just that dimension of sibling experience which I found so lacking in the empirical research—the symbolic and inner meaning. Indeed, except during the early period of his career when he was close to Freud, Jung rarely refers to actual infantile sibling interaction. At that time he wrote Freud a detailed account of his own eldest daughter's response to the birth of a baby brother that celebrates the many parallels between his Anna and Freud's "Little Hans" and how splendidly Anna's reactions confirmed Freud's theories about sibling jealousy and infantile sexuality. Yet even then Jung was especially interested in how the infant's arrival encouraged the older child's introversion and stimulated her imagination.

Anna's immediate answer to father Jung's asking, "What would you do if you got a little brother tonight?" is "I would kill him." She worries that her mother will disappear, accuses her of betrayal and deceit, challenges her to prove her love continues. Sleepless and afraid at night, she is obsessed with the question, "Where did this baby come from?" and distrustful of the stork story her father had given her. The explanations she herself devises are typical of what Freud called "the sexual theories of children." Even when her father gives her more accurate information, she exhibits a marked preference for her own fantastic, mythological explanations. Jung observes in his daughter what he celebrates as an important new feature: "reveries, the first stirrings of poetry, moods of an elegaic strain." The actual baby brother is balanced by a fantasy big brother "who knew everything, could do everything, and had everything," who is brave and invulnerable, whose relation to her parallels her father's relation to her mother. As Jung understands it, part of the libidinal energy that had formerly been directed outward is now turned inward and there produces increased fantasy activity. Jung comes to see this as the most important aspect: the demonstration of "the characteristic striving of the child's imagination to outgrow its 'realism' and to put a 'symbolic' interpretation in the place of scientific rationalism." The episode seems to him evidence that the phenomenon of symbolic transformation is a natural psychic process rather than a consequence of repression.[1]

Jung's more characteristic reflections on siblings focus on the *inner* life of *adults*. Jung rarely speaks directly of sisters or brothers but rather of inner figures called "shadow," "anima" and "animus." Yet, as we shall see, he often describes the "shadow" as inner brother, the "anima" as an inner sister. This does not mean that "shadow" and "anima/animus" are to be understood as introjects of experiences with actual brothers or sisters—for they are "archetypes;" that is, *a priori* ways of ordering experience that are given with our humanness, *there*, prior to experience, shaping it. Thus, in Jung's view, these archetypes in large measure shape our earliest responses to biological siblings. The inner is for Jung prior to the outer. "The unconscious," he maintains, "is always there beforehand as a system of inherited psychic functioning handed down from primeval times."[2] (Though we should not exaggerate here; Jung is also careful to acknowledge that an archetypal *image*, the concrete, particular representation, always reflects individual and cultural experience.)

Jung's image of the human self envisions the conscious part of the psyche, the ego, as but one of the persons that live within us. Becoming whole involves coming to know these other aspects of ourselves and establishing a vital relationship with them, acknowledging that they, too, are us. In all of us, he believes, there lives a relatively unknown same-sex figure who embodies those aspects of ourselves that the ego would like to disown— our cruelty, perhaps, or our shameful vulnerability—but that we can relatively easily be brought to accept. This same-sex other he calls our "shadow," for he believes that the various repressed, painful, and ugly aspects constellate to form a kind of subpersonality that may appear as a hostile figure in our dreams or that we may project onto others—but that actually belongs to us and without which we are so one-dimensional as to not be able even to cast a shadow.

More hidden, more inaccessible, is another figure, the "anima," which appears in male psychology as a contrasexual, feminine other self with all the mysterious, numinous, and ambivalent allure that the feminine seems to evoke in males. This figure serves as a psychopomp, a soul guide; she teaches a mode of apprehension that values depth, feeling, imaginal resonance, rather than logic and utility. Jung posits an equivalent contrasexual figure for female psychology, which he calls the "animus," which represents those masculine aspects of the psyche that in women are likely to be unconscious.

This typology evidently works for most Jungians, though recently women have begun to speak up more clearly about how less adequately it fits their experience than it seems to fit the experience of men. As I have sought to understand how Jungian theory can help illumine sibling experience I have come to a rather perverse conclusion: a conviction that a focus on sibling experience could enormously simplify Jungian theory and address some of the stumbling blocks that feminists particularly— but not only they—discover in its present formulations.

What I find problematic in Jungian theory is its dependence on outmoded stereotypes of what constitutes "masculinity" and "femininity," its assumption that contrasexuality plays the same role in the psychology of women as it does in the psychology of men, the ease with which its model of the individuation process can be understood as a linear schema, the absurd machinations (e.g., "the anima of her animus") that the theory invokes to account for the appearance of positive same-sex figures in our dreams or other imaginal experiences, especially when they seem to serve a psychopompic function.

What I value in Jungian theory is its recognition of the "archetypal" dimensions of human experience. James Hillman calls his re-visioning of Jungian theory "archetypal psychology," and my proposals might well bear the same designation—and would, I believe, in large measure be compatible with Hillman's perspective. Though I should make clear that when I say "archetypal" I do not mean to approve the essentialism or the universalism implied by some of Jung's own writing about archetypes. I mean simply the valuation of the imaginal and metaphorical "depths" of experience and the recognition that at that "depth" level our experience reveals typical, transpersonal features that connect us to other humans, both those we know only through myth and art and those we know directly, in a way that feels transformative.

Jung himself often affirmed that there is no definitive "list" of archetypes; that focusing on a particular group is simply a way of trying to help us see patterns and connections within our experience and between our experience and that of others. In his essay "Concerning the Archetypes and the Anima Concept," Jung discusses the real difficulties involved with any archetypal typology and acknowledges the danger involved in trying to put all polarities into a "sexual schema" (like anima/animus) by main force. The phenomenology presented in case material is so infinitely varied and ever changing that it seems utterly to defy our powers of classification. Yet, because we need to get beyond the phenomenology if we are to explore the relationships among archetypes, we have to content ourselves with a theoretical "as if."[3]

Jung's "as ifs" were ego and shadow, anima and animus. Much is illuminated by his choices—and much confused or obscured. I believe there might be real value in the *experiment* of backing off from the focus on the shadow and the anima and animus and beginning again, focusing on what directly appears, as Jung himself began. I propose the "as if" of considering the brother and the sister as primary archetypes—rather than trying to fit these figures when they appear into the shadow/syzygy typology—and discovering what is thereby brought into view. Jung himself wrote often of the mother archetype, occasionally of the father archetype. There is nothing radically heretical in the proposal, though it organizes the phenomena differently, brings together some that the more familiar typology separates and vice versa.

At least for *my* project—the desire to see how Jung's understanding of the psyche opens us to dimensions of sibling experience we might otherwise miss—I am confident it will yield more than it will obscure.

It might help to remember that Jung chose the term *shadow* because it is one of the words used in many cultures to refer to the psyche: "The essence of that which has to be realized and assimilated has been so trenchantly and so plastically expressed in poetic language by the word 'shadow' that it would be almost presumptuous not to avail oneself of this linguistic heritage." He reminds us how in many primitive cultures (as among the Greeks) the soul is identified with the shadow, the intangible living presence that accompanies us throughout life, becomes active in sleep and after death—our psyche. The shadow or shade is a ghostlike presence that has objective reality and that the conscious ego can engage in conversation. Because it is independent, it is also experienced as capricious and dangerous.[4]

It is easy to forget that the shadow, like all archetypes, is ambivalent, that it represents both potentially destructive and potentially creative energies. Yet, according to Jung, whether the shadow is friend or foe depends on us. The same figure that may initially appear to the ego as a shadow, as a dark, devalued, or denied alter ego, may later be recognized as a manifestation of the Self, the term Jung uses to encompass images that express the transcendent and numinous dimensions of our potential wholeness.

The shadow is relevant to our interest in siblings because Jung says that in myth and literature and in our dreams the shadow is most often represented as a brother. Jung is especially fascinated by what he calls "the motif of the two hostile brothers," a motif that he sees as emblematic of all antitheses, especially of the two opposite approaches to grappling with the powerful influence of the unconscious: denial or acceptance, literalism or mysticism. Consideration of the motif almost always leads Jung to the two brothers in E. T. A. Hoffman's tale *The Devil's Elixir*. Jung's interpretation of the tale shows that the protagonist's denial and dread of his malicious and sinister brother leads to rigidity and narrow-mindedness, to a violent inflexibility, the one-dimensionality of a "man without a shadow."[5]

Jung believes that the primary task for males at mid-life is often learning how to reconnect with this brother figure. The apparent impossibility stimulates regression back to childhood, but because the means that worked then are of no avail, the regression continues beyond even early infancy into the legacy of ancestral life. Then mythological images, archetypes, are awakened, and an interior spiritual world whose existence was entirely unsuspected reveals itself. The confrontation with the archetypal shadow is like a primordial experience of the non-ego, an engagement with an interior opponent who throws down a challenge that initiates us into the labor of coming to terms with the unconscious.

Yet Jung's deepest reflections on the inner meaning of brotherhood are inspired not by antagonistic brothers but by the Greek Dioscuri, the twin brothers, one mortal, the other immortal, so devoted to one another they are unwilling to be separated even in death. In his essay on the rebirth archetype Jung writes:

> We are that pair of Dioscuri, one of whom is mortal and the other immortal, and who, though always together can never be made completely one. . . . We should prefer to be always "I" and nothing else. But we are confronted with that inner friend or foe, and whether he is our friend or foe depends on ourselves.

Jung sees in the mythological representations of friendship between two men an outer reflection of a relationship to that inner friend of the soul into whom Nature would like to change us— that other person who we are and yet can never completely become, that larger and greater personality maturing within us, the Self.[6]

As we reflect on this inner same-sex figure who may be either positive or negative, who is shadow or Self, it becomes evident that Jung's conception of the inner brother has much in common with the figure that Otto Rank calls the "Double." In his early work *The Myth of the Birth of the Hero,* as in his later voluminous study of the incest motif in myth and literature, Rank explored the importance of the hostile brother motif as a recurrent mythological and literary theme. Often the brothers are twins, and often one must die to assure the other's life. In his later writings Rank subsumes this motif under that of the Double. The brother is now seen as primarily an inner figure, an alter ego. The Double may represent either the mortal or the immortal self, may be feared as image of one's mortality or prized as signifying one's imperishability. The Double is Death or the Immortal Soul. It inspires fear and love, arouses the "eternal conflict" between our "need for likeness and desire for difference." The Double answers to the need for a mirror, a shadow, a reflection. It seems to take on an independent life but is so intimately bound to the hero's vital being that misfortune befalls him if he tries to detach himself too completely from it.

Rank reminds us that the primitive "considers the shadow his mysterious double, a spiritual yet real being" and that the Greek name for such a shadowlike double—for that aspect of the self which survives in death and which is active in dream when the conscious ego has withdrawn—was *psyche*. Thus for Rank the relationship to an inner same-sex sibling, to a double, comes to signify relationship to one's unconscious self, one's psyche, and to both death and immortality. At its deepest it expresses our longing to let the ego die and to be united with a transcendent self. It signifies our longing for surrender to something larger than ego.

The image of sibling love represents our urge to move "beyond psychology." The first phase of psychic life proceeds by way of differentiation, often manifesting as hostility, but the second phase is accomplished through surrender and love. Yet Rank warns of the danger of taking this literally, externally. No human other, spouse or sibling, can bear the burden of playing the role of alter ego for another. "This reaching out for something bigger . . . originates in the individual's need for expansion beyond the realm of his self, . . . for some kind of 'beyond' . . . to which he can submit." But there is nothing in reality that "can carry the weight of this expansion." It is enormously difficult "to realize that there exists a difference between one's spiritual and one's purely human needs, and that the satisfaction or fulfillment for each has to be found in different spheres." The false personalizing of the need to be loved inevitably precipitates despair and the feeling of irredeemable inferiority. Rank hopes to help us recognize that the image of the complementing, completing double is a symbol that no human other can incarnate for us; we need to understand it religiously; to see it as embodying our dual need for differentiation and likeness, for individuality and connection, for natural life and immortality. His reflection on the sibling motif takes him "beyond psychology."[7]

At times Jung's conception of the shadow is equally profound; at other times he writes as though from the ego's perspective and sees the shadow as a negative figure, as embodiment simply of the devalued and denied aspects of our personal history that we must reintegrate before we are ready for the real work of individuation, which proceeds through engagement with the contra-sexual archetypes. The last stage of the journey to psychological wholeness, as Jung describes it, again involves an archetype that appears as a same-sex figure, the Self. The model, when presented in this linear form, radically separates the engagements with the two inner same-sex figures, the shadow and the Self—one belongs to the beginning of the journey, the other to its end. The inner bond between shadow and Self is thus often obscured. The numinosity and ambivalence inherent in this same-sex figure are what we would expect if we simply spoke of him as our inner brother.

Not too surprisingly Jung writes more often about the meaning of brother imagery for men than about the meaning of sister imagery for women. The most extended discussion of the latter appears in an essay about the case of a ten-year-old disabled girl who had become so stuck in an identification with her physical and moral inferiority that she had become much more infantile than her actual handicaps warranted and seemingly incapable of extricating herself. "Such a condition is most favorable to the growth of a second personality. The fact that her conscious mind fails to progress does not mean in the least that her unconscious personality will also remain at a standstill. This part of herself will advance as time goes on, and the more the conscious part hangs back, the greater will be the dissociation of personality. Then one day the more developed personality will appear on the scene and challenge the regressive ego." This is just what happened with this particular patient, who one day during the course of therapy announced that she had an imaginary twin sister. This sister for a time served as an embodiment of that in the child which was healthy and growing. "Later the two merged into one, and this signified a tremendous advance, enabling the girl to begin to take responsibility for her own difficulties."[8]

Even more important to Jung than the inner confrontation

with the same-sex sibling is the engagement with the contra-sexual inner figure that he calls anima in men and animus in women. Initially, he says, this factor in men is identical with the mother-imago and is taken to be the real mother. Jung believes that to work free of absorption by the mother archetype requires the appearance of another female figure, one who can be experienced on a more equal plane, one with whom one can establish a mutual, reciprocal relation. "The projection can only be dissolved when the son sees that in the realm of his psyche there is an image not only of the mother but of the daughter, the sister, the beloved." Dreams announcing a shift whereby the sister replaces the mother as the source of life represent the dreamer's being freed from domination by unconscious and infantile attitudes. "The mother is superior to the son, but the sister is his equal." When the anima assumes this sister shape she becomes a life-giving force.[9]

In Jung's later work his focus shifts from symbolic mother-son incest to symbolic brother-sister incest, which is for him representative of an inner marriage of ego and anima. He comes to regard the mother-son relationship as relevant only to the initial stage of psychological transformation: the moment of rebirth. But the individuation process is a lifelong task, more adequately symbolized by the brother-sister relationship. Jung views the holy wedding (the *hieros gamos*) between divine or royal brother and sister as one of the most satisfying images of individuation (along with the image of the hermaphrodite, brother and sister become one). Jung sees the mother of the earlier phase as naturally transformed into the sister-spouse of the more mature engagement. Because the son emerges from his incestuous reunion with the mother as her spouse, the continuation of the process leads to the spontaneous appearance of images of the *hieros gamos*, the sacred and forbidden, intensely intimate union of brother and sister. That such a marriage is taboo if understood literally forces us to discover the image's symbolic meaning; we learn that the longed-for *coniunctio* means the urge toward wholeness, toward union with Self.[10]

I suspect that the understanding of the inner meaning of the brother-sister relationship put forward by Jung may be more relevant to the psychology of men than of women, may (not too surprisingly) reflect the brother's experience of the relationship. Jung's conception of the anima and his conviction that a contra-sexual figure serves the male as the guide to his soul derives from his own experience and corresponds to the experience of his male patients. But, as Jung himself acknowledges, his con-ception of the animus was originally derived as a logical deduc-tion from male experience rather than from his work with women, and many of his female patients and students remained discontent with the formulation. It wasn't that they didn't have dreams and other important imaginal experiences in which brother/lover figures appear but that these figures did not seem to carry the same meaning that the sister/lover carried for male psychology. The animus figure might represent some important psychological attributes traditionally deemed "masculine" that were not fully integrated into the woman's conscious personality. The task of assimilating this figure might, indeed, be an impor-tant individuation labor. But the animus was not an image of the woman's own soul as anima seemed to be for men.[11]

"Soul images of women," as Irene Claremont de Castillejo discovered, were female.[12] This suggests that for women the sister/lover cannot easily be seen only as a shadow but rather figures in their psychology much as the anima figures in the psychology of men. The sister may function as both shadow and soul for women, whereas it may be that for men the figure of the brother represents the shadow and that of the sister the soul—though as we indicated earlier, at times Jung sees how for men the brother, too, might serve as soul image.

Of course, Jung himself never suggests that a woman might have an anima, that a same-sex figure might function in her psychology as a contra-sexual one does in the psychology of men, that for both women and men the sister might appear as the most important psychopomp. Yet in his essay on the Kore, the maiden figure of Greek mythology, he recognizes that the same image might represent both the anima in male psychology and the self or "supraordinate personality" in the psychology of women. Although Jung ends up discussing the Kore archetype mostly as an anima projection, he acknowledges the inadequacy, indeed the inappropriateness, of this approach. He perceives that the myth is clearly essentially a feminine one centered on a female-female relationship that is alien to men and shuts them out. Yet when trying to understand what the Kore archetype might mean to women, he considers Kore only in terms of her relation with Demeter, only in terms of mother-daughter bonding, as daughter not as maiden. Thus he misses the opportunity to explore what role the relation to the inner maiden might have in the psychology of women.[13]

Jungians rarely write explicitly about our interactions with literal others, about our relationships with the familial parents or our actual siblings. When they do, it is usually to demonstrate the importance of moving to the recognition that our real engagement must be with the archetypal mother not the accidental carrier of the archetype, with the archetypal brother or sister.

I think, for example, of Esther Harding's discussion of sisterhood. She writes of the identification that often binds sisters to one another so closely that they may even dream the same dreams. They may fall in love with the same man—often without knowing of one another's involvement—or men who turn out to be very alike despite striking overt dissimilarities. Such closely enmeshed sisters are likely to attempt to differentiate by emphasizing external differences, by taking clearly defined complementary roles; in reality this discrimination is but further evidence of their identification. "Else why should not each sister be free to function on any or all sides of life?" Neither of the sisters is a whole individual but only a part of the family. Each "is identified with the other sister who together with herself make up a completed whole. In such cases no psychological relationship is possible, for relationship implies separateness." Harding believes that the energy that is still fixated on a sister, and so held unseen and unrecognized in the unconscious, must be freed and applied to conscious development. "She does not feel inferior today because years ago in her schoolroom days her sister was bigger than she was; she feels inferior *today* because part of her psyche has remained undeveloped." Thus Harding is pointing to how the very process that may have been essential in childhood for ego development must be redone at a different level in adulthood; now the inner sister must be made conscious and a relationship established to *her.* The pull to redo things with the outward sister may be evasion of a far more compelling task.[14] I agree—and yet believe that the focus on the inner sister may also sometimes be evasion.

Most Jungians have worked uncritically with the theoretical terms introduced by Jung. His increasing emphasis in his later years on the importance of moving beyond a psychology dominated by the mother archetype has been ignored by almost everyone other than James Hillman, for whom it has been a central theme. Hillman believes that when the concern for soul is paramount, relationship cannot take the hierarchical form of the parent-child connection but must base itself instead on the model of the brother-sister pair, a model that implies the mutuality of soul-making. It is reciprocal and equal love for one another's psychic development that is creative. His reading of the "Amor and Psyche" tale expresses his conviction that what heals is our need for each other, mutuality not mothering. What heals is not consciousness but the capacity to love.[15]

Hillman encourages me to explore how a psychology that focuses on the archetypes of the sister and brother might help us toward a deeper understanding of soul-making—and might also help us move beyond the convolutions that Jung's preferred phenomenology sometimes seems to require of us. As I have already noted, Jung's conception of the shadow tends too easily, to my mind, to be taken in a way that ignores the ambivalence of all archetypes. Subsuming all same-sex figures under this archetype then leads to convoluted manipulations about the relation between shadow and Self. Similarly, subsuming all contra-sexual figures under the anima-animus archetype fails to help us disentangle the differences between the role of the anima in male psychology and that of the animus in female psychology.

Jung never directly modifies his insistence on the centrality of contra-sexuality in the psychology of both men and women. His own psychological theory continues to focus on the *coniunctio oppositoriuim,* on polarities and complementarities. He acknowledges that in its quiescent, unprojected state the *coniunctio* archetype has no exactly determinable form, but nevertheless regards anima-animus as a privileged representation for the whole conception of opposites: dry-moist, hot-cold, male-female, sun-moon, gold-silver, round-square, water-fire, physical-spiritual. Jung does note that the alchemists from whom so much of his psychological language derives were discontent with the marriage symbolism and continually felt obliged to make use of other "uniting symbols" that did not depend on contra-sexuality: a dragon embracing a woman in a grave, two animals fighting, a king dissolving in water.[16]

Hillman has recognized the importance of trying to move beyond a psychology dominated by contra-sexual assumptions, beyond a psychology that images psychic wholeness in terms of androgyny, an inner union of male and female aspects of the self. His work on the "senex-puer constellation" in male psychology shows the importance of same-sex relationships as images for psychic wholeness. Though this constellation pairs an older male with a younger one, they are not father and son. Indeed, the most obvious mythological figuration is that of divine brotherhood, infant Hermes tricking elder brother Apollo, Hermes as adult tenderly holding Dionysos as babe.[17]

I see Patricia Berry's re-visioning of the shadow archetype as giving us a new way to understand same-sex, that is, sister-sister, images in female psychology. She, too, is moving beyond a psychology dominated by contra-sexuality, by the fantasy of opposites. Her suggestion that the relationship between ego and shadow is constantly shifting like the reversible relation between figure and ground seems highly relevant to the complex and subtle mutuality of the sister bond, where either sister can be viewed as the ego-figure. She also sees how the opposition between the two is not simply a *moral* one, not simply the relation of a "good" figure to an evil one. Shadows in painting, she observes, are not usually black but a deeper shade of the same color; colors that clash are not those from opposite sides of the spectrum but those close to each other, like pink and red. It is the *shades* of difference that are most felt. She also writes of how we may use polarities to achieve "balances" that conveniently serve to keep us out of the depths. The psychology of the shadow may itself encourage a dangerous reducing, simplifying, literalizing of opposites.[18]

Sisters are like the subtle shadows Berry points to: the

importance of the actual other sister is that she is too "other" to be easily integrated through the neat trick of polarization. The inner sister, too, serves as symbol of that which can always still undermine the ego no matter how well balanced. The shadow as an abstract theoretical concept is not threatening, as it is in its particular actual appearances. The specific, intimate, small, unexpected ways in which the sister appears in our lives wounds and challenges, creates the tension that forces consciousness and change—as Psyche's sisters were just the sisters to provoke *her* toward consciousness.

Hillman has also written powerfully of the need to reexamine Jung's conception of the anima and animus. He believes that for men understanding anima in terms of contra-sexuality leads to sentimental pieties about saving soul through relationships and about becoming more feminine. For women it means denial of soul, denial that for them, too, the shift toward interiority is task not given, and a misleading misinterpretation of all female images as shadow. In Jung's schema, the same image might be ennobled as a man's anima and denigrated as a woman's shadow. Hillman proposes instead that for both men and women the relation to anima means a way of perceiving and behaving "that gives events the significance of soul," that discovers the *depth* dimension, the imaginal significance, within the profane.[19] Hillman is seeking, as Jung had also, to break out of the false polarity of inner and outer worlds. Anima-consciousness means relating with soul to the outer world, not relating to our own subjectivity. Anima is "Sister Soul" for both women and men. The sister bond, deliteralized, serves to further soul-making.

Thus there have been some explorations within the Jungian tradition of how a psychology centering on brother and sister might constellate psyche. We need, however, to be able to imagine more concretely, more sensuously, more variously, how these archetypes actually function in our lives. It is not enough to say, "Let's move beyond a psychology dominated by the mother archetype and by contra-sexuality; let's move to a psychology that considers sister and brother as primary archetypes." The myths we looked at earlier supply the necessary "fleshing out"; they make evident the variety of ways in which brothers and sisters—inner and outer—appear in our lives.

Jung's psychology provides that recognition of the inner and symbolic significance of primary relationships that more extroverted and behavioral approaches ignore, but at the cost of disregarding the complex interplay between inner and outer that seems to constitute our actual lives. The Jungian assumption is clearly that what happens within is more real, that is, more valuable, more important, than what happens between. I have saved Freud to consider after Jung because I see his psychology as doing more justice to the interplay between inner and outer and between contemporary experience and mythological paradigm—and also because the feminist writers I want to include respond more directly and more passionately to the work of Freud than to that of Adler or of Jung.

9. Oedipus' Sisters

It may be difficult to realize the degree to which it is Freud's influence that underlies our twentieth-century focus on mother-child relationships as the most formative and powerful of all human bonds. Yet, as George Steiner points out in his *Antigones,* during the nineteenth century it was Sophokles' *Antigone* with its stunning dramatization of sister-brother devotion that was looked upon as the paradigmatic Greek tragedy, the tragedy that explored the deepest undercurrents of human experience.[1] Freud's *Interpretation of Dreams* changed all that.

Still we should remember that in Freud's first published discussion of Sophokles' hero, he focused as much on Oedipus' search for self-knowledge as on his fulfillment of our repressed longings for our mother's love.[2] In *Oedipus Rex* the blind seer Teiresias is the one who really sees; in *Oedipus at Colonus* the self-blinded Oedipus, dependent on Antigone's eyes, has during his years of exiled wandering come to see the true nature of his own fate. True sight, insight, is sister-sight. In his later years Freud speaks more often of Oedipus' relation to his sister/daughter Antigone than to his mother/wife Jocasta—admittedly, in large measure a function of his ongoing personal identification with the ancient Greek hero. He, Sigmund, the one of the victorious mouth, is now (after his cancer operation had made all speech awkward and painful and public speaking an impossibility) dependent on his daughter, his Anna/Antigone, to be his mouth.[3] Those references to Antigone symbolize how central a role sibling experience actually plays in psychoanalysis, in this Oedipus-dominated psychology.

Depth psychology begins with the son, with Freud's discovery that like Oedipus he harbors incestual longings for his mother and parricidal resentment of his father. Freud never overcomes his assumption that male experience, filial experience, is the paradigm of all human experience; women *are* for him deficient, castrated males. Yet in the 1920s he begins to see that female sexual development is not symmetrical with male, that the female infant's earliest attachment is not contra-sexual but homosexual, that for girls as well as for boys the first love-object is the mother. Although he recognizes that this means that for females all subsequent same-sex relationships will evoke the intense ambivalence associated with this primary bond, he has nothing specific to say about how this might affect the relationship between sisters. Freud acknowledges that the importance of the daughter's attachment to the mother was long hidden from him, because so seldom reenacted in the transference relationship as played out between his female patients and himself, a male analyst. It was the testimony of the early female analysts that first alerted him to the importance of this "Minoan-Mycenaean" pre-Oedipal phase. But attachments between sisters *remain* invisible.[4]

Although Freud's psychology encompasses much more than a new insistence on the importance of the mother to both male and female children, although it admits to the central significance of sibling interaction—his psychology nevertheless remains a psychology of the *son*. Indeed (as Adler made evident), it was always a psychology seen from the perspective of the eldest son, the son who is to begin with the only son. Thus Freud sees fraternal relationships primarily in terms of rivalry for parental attention and affection. He assumes that relationships among siblings are shaped by the prior importance for each of their ties to their parents. It never occurs to him that for later children the sibling, too, is already there, is part of his first world.

So much of Freud's genius derives from his seemingly unquestioned assumption of the archetypal universality of his own experience that it should not surprise us that here, too, much of what Freud has to say about the murderous hatred that children feel toward a younger, intruding sibling can be connected to what he was willing to disclose about his response to the birth of his next younger brother—and to the guilt he felt when that brother died in infancy. The genius and the limitations of Freud's world both derive from his having been his own most important patient.

In trying to understand Freud it is important to remember that there is a sense in which he is not speaking of childhood experience in the literal sense at all. What he says about infancy derives from the psychoanalytic interpretations of the contemporary dreams and retrospective memories of adults—memories that he looks upon as being always to some degree imaginal rather than factual. Although much of what he says about childhood has subsequently been confirmed by the work of child analysts like Melanie Klein, Freud's interest was really in the influence on our lives in the present of our childhood as it persists in our conscious and unconscious memory.

In us as adults the urgent desires and fears of our childhood selves are still alive, influencing our present actions and feelings to a degree few of us would admit. The reason for Freud's insistence on the universal relevance of the Oedipus myth was to bring us to recognize the lifelong persistence of the intensity of those impulses that haunted the Theban king—our childish longings to have all the other's love for ourself, to eliminate all rivals. The myth speaks to us because it speaks about us. Nor is the Oedipus myth the only one Freud viewed as in some way a component of our own psyches. His fascination with Narcissus and with Psyche, with Eros, Death, and Ananke, express his sense of the relevance of these myths to our experience. The "Elektra complex" was originally Jung's idea, not Freud's, and Freud soon discarded it because its adoption had been inspired by the rejected notion that male and female experience were symmetrical. Yet Freud would have agreed that we "are" Elektra and Ismene, Orestes and Polyneices, and not only Oedipus. Those bizarre and frightening deeds that permeated the sibling myths we have looked at—eating one's own children, cutting out tongues, leaving corpses to be eaten by dogs, murdering one's brother—may seem far, indeed, from anything we could even imagine doing, but our dreams suggest otherwise.

Freud helps us recall the passionate ambivalence of our earliest emotional attachments—the complex intertwining of love and hatred, wish and fear—and, less obviously perhaps, of our adult ones as well. He also helps us to understand why so often what we do is the opposite of what we wanted; aversion and desire so easily supplant each other. He helps us see how in later life we turn to those with whom we are intimate with the same unfulfilled longings and the same unappeased dread that motivated us in infancy. "Transference" does not happen only in analysis but in all significant relationships. Nor do we "transfer" only our infantile dispositions toward our parents; there are also sister and brother transferences. Freud's conviction of our original "bisexuality," his belief that all of us respond in both "masculine" and "feminine" ways irrespective of our biological sex, also yields a complex understanding of our relationships—I, a woman (for example), might act as brother to my sister!

Analysis, so Freud believes, can lead us toward the kind of self-understanding that Oedipus comes to represent, toward the separation of past from present, fantasy from fact. It can teach us that fantasy become conscious adds depth, multidimensionality, to our experience, whereas the unconscious confusion of imagination and "reality" brings only suffering and bewilderment.

Freud believed that all of us are influenced by primal fantasies that feel like memories but are at work in us independent of the historical particularities of our individual experience.[5] His explicit listing of such primal fantasies includes witnessing parental intercourse, suffering paternal seduction, and being threatened with castration—but sibling experience seems also to belong on the list. Irrespective of what "actually" happened, we "remember" watching our parents make love—which means that we were already *there*, are not dependent on them for our very existence; we "remember" hearing them make love and forever after see pain and joy as deeply interfused. We "remember" being made love to by the parent we so deeply desired and whose power we so fearfully dreaded. We "remember" being threatened with impotence, with nonexistence, and "remember" stealing our parent's power for ourselves. If we were only children, we "remember" playing with the sibling who alleviated our aloneness, and if we had siblings, we "remember" getting rid of the one who dared to challenge our cherished "onlyness."

Freud describes how our literal experience of our brothers or sisters is filled out with imaginary creatures, with secret playmates and with threatening monsters hiding in the mother's womb—or by the fear that one's longing to stay "only" killed the potential rivals even before they were born. For Freud siblings exist in our psychic, inner life irrespective of whether we literally had brothers or sisters. Because siblings play such a central role in our imaginal life, they are included among those very few things that function as tenor (the latent meaning of a manifest image) in symbolic representation:

> The range of things which are given symbolic representation in dreams is not wide: the human body as a whole, parents, children, brothers and sisters, birth, death, nakedness. . . . and sexual life—the genitals, sexual processes, sexual intercourse.[6]

The most common manifest images that when interpreted signify brothers and sisters are, according to Freud, small animals—helpful animals like bees and ants to represent the positive side of the relationship, vermin (disgusting, annoying, or noxious small animals that prey on game and are difficult to control) to stand for the despicable aspect.

As I have reread Freud in the light of my interest in sibling experience, I am surprised to discover how great an importance he attributes to it. How easily our response to his focus on mother-child relationship seems to blind us to other dimensions of his thought. Yet in Freud's view some of the most significant moments in our psychological development are associated with interactions among sisters and brothers. As he portrays it, our embryonic ego awareness, the emergence of our gender identity, our earliest intellectual and imaginal activity are all engendered by sibling experience.

Sibling interaction is seen by Freud as closely interwoven with the beginning of consciousness, of psychic life. There is a before—the pre-Oedipal period—but the beginnings of ego awareness, our earliest memories, are often intimately associated with the stirrings of hostile feelings toward a sibling. Freud interprets a childhood recollection of Goethe's—a memory of throwing pottery dishes out the window—as signifying the future poet's longing to get rid of a much resented younger sibling.[7] The first experience of "I" and "other" may come not vis-à-vis the mother but in relation to a sibling; separation, autonomy, may seem less threatening, less of an all-or-nothing issue, in relation to a sibling than to the all-powerful mother.

Elsewhere Freud attributes the first impetus toward intellectual activity to the sexual curiosity inspired by the birth of a new sibling. This resented event leads the older child to ask: "Where did this baby come from, and how do I prevent such an occurrence from happening again?" Thus Freud believes that our questioning about human origins is not originally a question about our own origin. Our own existence is to begin with taken for granted and only becomes contingent with our discovery of the new infant's source.[8] I remember vividly how true this was for my sons.

Freud also suggests that jealous feelings toward siblings may be connected to the beginning of imaginal creativity. The first highly elaborated conscious fantasy is often what Freud called the "family romance," the fancy that I am an adopted child, that my true parents who really love me are much more wonderful and powerful than the pitiable ones who are raising me and whose true worthlessness has been revealed with the arrival of the clearly inferior new infant who is undeniably their child.[9] How well I recall my own version of this, which was inspired not by the birth of my first sibling, my brother, but by that of my sister when I was four. The stories I made up about my "real" family were the ones I told in the nursery when we were supposed to be asleep—my first experience of the still relished pleasure of story telling.

Jealous rivalry for parental regard is seen by Freud as the leitmotif of sibling interaction. He emphasizes the intensity and ruthlessness of the child's hostility to its sibling. The hatred is expressed not only in disparaging remarks but in "murderous assaults." Though the enmity may later be overlaid by a more affectionate attitude, it nevertheless persists, revealing its continued life in dreams. Because children can much more easily afford to hate a sibling than a parent on whom they are utterly dependent and because they often discover that the expression of negative feelings toward siblings is treated matter-of-factly by their parents, they make little attempt to hide or disguise the hostility.[10]

I find especially provocative Freud's suggestion that although children seem to make something "sacred" of the parent-child relation, they see the bond between brothers and sisters as "profane."[11] I find this a powerful way of expressing that the two relationships are experienced as taking place on different planes, as being essentially incommensurate. This may help explain why children seem unafraid that a particular act of hostility toward a sibling will be reified, why it seems self-evident to them that their hatred is compatible with the love they also feel and are likely to express just a few minutes later.

Yet Freud believes that as children come to recognize that their parents do love the other child, they realize that maintaining their hostile attitude will only damage themselves. Thus—although the bond among the siblings is still based on their common love for the mother and the father—they learn to identify with the other children, to replace their jealousy with "group feeling." We are all in the same situation and thus all equal. If I cannot be the favorite, then no one can; all must be the same and have the same. Freud views this renunciation of competition as the model for all communal feelings, all social bonding.[12] Sibling experience initiates us into Eros, into the love of others *as* other, on which civilization depends. In the myth of the primal parricide, which Freud recounts in *Totem and Taboo,* this understanding of "group psychology" as a derivative of sibling experience is explicit: the mythic brothers initially bond together out of their shared resentment of the father; then, released from his authority and free to compete with one another, they rediscover their love of the father, acknowledge their shared guilt, and abjure the rivalry that might otherwise destroy them.[13]

In Freud's view *same-sex* siblings inspire especially intense rivalry and identification. He suggests that sometimes a boy's excessively hostile infantile feelings toward a brother later yield to a transformation whereby the rival of the earlier period becomes the first homosexual love object. Of the many possible etiologies for male homosexuality introduced in Freud's writings—at various times he emphasizes the early relation to the father, the mother, the sister, or the brother—Freud sees the last as most likely to be marked "by a special development of the social instincts and by a devotion to the interests of the community."[14]

Despite Freud's emphasis on brother-brother interaction, he

also acknowledges the psychological importance of brother-sister relationships. Freud attributes the first awareness of gender identity to infantile interactions with a sibling of the opposite sex. The boy's discovery that his sister has no penis initates him into the castration fear that will thereafter haunt his experience of his own masculinity. The girl's discovery that she has no penis (which Freud believes she experiences as loss, as already effected castration) introduces her to that envy of male sexuality and privilege that he sees as central to feminine psychosexuality. This discovery leads her both to recognize her affinity with her mother and, wishing she could disavov her own femininity, to repudiate her mother. For both girl and boy the discovery of difference stirs fear.[15]

Freud also writes of the brother or sister as the first surrogate love objects; in learning to love the sister in place of the unavailable mother, the brother in place of the father, we for the first time participate in that sequence of loss, mourning, replacement, that will be required of us over and over again. This is our first lesson in substitution, symbolization, sublimation, and the acceptance of finitude.[16]

Noting how often, though forbidden in actuality, brother-sister incest is celebrated among the gods and required of royalty, Freud infers that brother-sister incest may represent a universal longing that, like Oedipal desire, is to be assuaged neither through repression nor literal fulfillment but through interpretation, through acknowledgement and consciously substitutionery fulfillment. Freud's interpretations suggest that this incestuous longing represents the male's unconscious admission of his bisexuality and his longing to embrace his own femininity. For males the relation to the sister is emblematic of the relation to their own denied passivity and mortality. This association between the themes of sisterhood and death is, as we have already noted, focal in Freud's discussion of the Psyche story and of fairy tales.[17]

How much we miss of the depth of Freud's sense of the role of sibling experience in the development of human consciousness if we reduce his insights to "sibling rivalry." Our discovery of our own autonomy, our awareness of being a female or male person, our earliest experiences of our capacity to learn and to imagine are, in Freud's view, often associated with early sibling interaction. I am especially moved by his intuition of how engagement with the sister is what leads us to psyche, to psychological awareness, and to a coming to terms with the inevitability of our own death. He writes of this as true for men; I believe it is true for women as well, that for us also it is the sister, not the brother, who provides access to the most profound layers of human experience.

Yet in all that Freud writes about siblings he never touches on the relation of sister to sister. The relation of mother to daughter had long been hidden from him, but *this* relation is even more hidden. (When Freud first examined female homosexuality he interpreted it primarily in terms of father-rejection; in his late essays he saw it as a return to the primary love object, the mother, but it seems never to have occurred to him to propose a genesis in early sister-sister feeling parallel to the form of male homosexuality based on infantile fraternal feeling.) Freud admitted that his access to the significance of mother-daughter bonding had been inhibited by his being a male analyst and so mostly receiving father-transference. Yet Freud confided to H.D. how often he had been the object of a mother transference (and admitted how awkward and confusing that was to him).[18] Since it is not likely that he was ever aware of receiving a sister transference, he probably never had even such indirect access to sister-sister relationship.

Nor does he seem to have been pulled to try to understand from within the character of the relationships among his own five sisters (who had had to yield so much privilege to him when they were all children) or that between his wife, Martha, and her sister, Minna, who lived with the Freuds during most of their marriage, or that among his own three daughters.[19] The undeniable reality of sisterly bonds as part of Freud's everyday experience and yet their essential invisibility to him suggests repression, suggests that the relationship is fearful to men, perhaps even more terrifying than the mother-daughter relation. Perhaps intimate peer involvements between women may suggest to men that women do not need men as much as men need women.

For there is an "under-text" to what Freud writes about the

psychology of women that we must uncover if we are to take full advantage of what psychoanalysis could help us to see about women, about sisters. Because Freud wrote about women from his own, male perspective his psychology of women is, as it cannot help but be, "a deposit of the desires and disappointments of men." (The phrase is Karen Horney's.) What Freud gives us are male fantasies about women, male fears of women and their dependence on women (particularly on the mother who gave them birth), male fears of becoming women and thus losing their vaunted autonomy. As we read Freud as Freud taught us to read, we easily see the latent meanings of the surface affirmations: womb envy is the underside of penis-envy; the denied truth of male contingency is the underside of the insistence on female inferiority, the longing for fusion and quiescence the underside of the valorization of autonomy and activity. The designation of male experience as the paradigm of all human experience is recognized as manifestly a reaction formation!

To understand the role that sisters play in the psychology of women we must begin from our own female perspective. We must go beyond Freud. Yet in doing so we should give Freud our thanks, for it is he who has taught us to look for such undertexts and much about how to read them. In articulating a feminist perspective—though many feminists, of course, find nothing useful in Freud at all—Freud (as I have come to understand him) faces us as a brother who both helps and hinders. In moving beyond Freud, we use Freud against Freud.

10. Feminism's Sisters

So, what *has* feminism had to say about sisters? My first impulse is to respond: Nothing! And, though this is, of course, an exaggeration, it nonetheless expresses my disappointment. Although feminists have written often enough about the power and beauty of "sisterhood," they have rarely acknowledged those actualities of kinship experience that underlie the metaphor. Consequently their paeans sound thin and unconvincing—and have little prepared us for the ambivalences that seem inevitably to intrude when women bond deeply with women.

I subscribe enough to Freud's view of our humanness to agree with him that such ambivalence is an almost inescapable correlate of any deeply emotional human relationship, any relationship that recalls the primary attachments of childhood—and, clearly, when we say "sisterhood" we imply that we *mean,* indeed, that we *desire,* such invocation. However, the sister bond also stirs up ambivalences peculiar to this particular relationship, ambivalences associated with the ways in which the sister-sister relationship is like that other primary female-female connection, the bond between mothers and daughters—and different from it. An awareness that adult relationships among women are likely to stir up "sister stuff" should alert us to some particular probable difficulties—as well as prepare us to enjoy to full advantage the positive possibilities.

In recent years the most sophisticated feminist theorists have, in their reflections on the psychology of women, focused almost exclusively on the mother-daughter relationship. Much has been brought to light by their work—and much left obscure by their neglect of the relationship between sisters.

But let us begin by seeing what women have had to say about female psychology that might be relevant to our understanding of sister-sister and sisterlike experience.

Among the women associated with Freud during the 1920s,

the women who helped Freud to discover the salience of mother-daughter attachments, was Helene Deutsch, who wrote extensively about the psychology of women. In her work she recognized the importance of the sister relation in the psychology of women, although, interestingly, she subsumes it under "two-girl friendships" rather than seeing the friendships as a variant of or surrogate for the sister bond. This seems to be because she believes that sister feeling (especially the ideal part) is usually transferred from the sister even when there is one—as though the actual sister is inevitably experienced as falling short of the ideal, as being unworthy of the archetype.

Deutsch suggests that these surrogate friendships appeal because they enable the young girl to evade the ambivalence always present in primary relationships. Deutsch attributes enormous importance to these sister*like* bonds, especially in early adolescence, a period of shared sexual curiosity and investigation. (Though there may be homosexual tenderness between the girls, Deutsch says, she believes there is rarely physical, genital contact.) This female intimate serves as a double; a mutual process of identification helps each achieve the sense of a separate ego. Deutsch sees this as a kind of mutual seduction that is especially important in helping each to effect the necessary separation from the mother. Deutsch views the sister figure, not the brother, as the one with whose help the girl discovers the character of her own femininity and comes to accept it. But according to Deutsch it is from men that females really learn about their own sexuality; it is they who help us to discover our unknown vagina and to value it; they who make possible the only genuinely fulfilling feminine experience: maternity. We learn who we are from the other, from the one who is different, not from the one who is like us.

As Deutsch sees the normal pattern, in late adolescence, as the girl turns her erotic interest toward males, the sisterly friendship loses its centrality and power. The turn from sister-figure to brother-figure recapitulates what Freud had posited about the turn from mother to father—and is as precarious; the girl may instead develop more overt homosexual interests. Deutsch leaves no room for intense relationships with sisters or sister surrogates in the lives of normal women in maturity, for she assumes that all their libidinal energy is focused on "motherhood"—as all sexual pleasure for women is maternal. (Even orgasm is from Deutsch's perspective pleasurable only because it serves as analogue for parturition.) Not surprisingly, there is no sense in Deutsch that a woman might have any real life after her childbearing years are over. The real coming to terms with death in the lives of women comes at menopause. After that a woman is of no further use to herself or her species. It never occurs to Deutsch that this might be a time for overcoming the imbalance caused by years of compulsive heterosexuality. The relationship with women belongs only to a fixed phase in a woman's life—only as preparation for motherhood.[1] (Although in other respects her psychology of women deviates more from Freud's than does Deutsch's, on this point Clara Thompson agrees: the early pubertal intimacy among girls is very important because the ability to love a same-sex other is the first real experience of object love and serves as an important basis for being able to love heterosexually.)[2]

Another of the early female analysts to write on women's psychology was Karen Horney. Her comments on sister-sister experience emphasize the lifelong damage that passionate sisterly relationships during childhood may engender. She believes that early sibling sexual play—especially the seduction of a younger sister by an older—may provoke fear and resentment that persist throughout a lifetime. Intense infantile sister relationships issue in violent adult hostility toward women, which may be manifested either in exaggerated competition or in equally exaggerated evasion of competition with women. Horney attributes female resistance in therapy to a negative sister transference; the resistance represents a reanimation of early childhood rivalry with an elder sister, a reawakening of the rage felt at the sister's having won the competition for a man's love (i.e., the love of their father or brother), and, particularly, anger at her having done so through her femininity.[3]

All of these female theorists seem to assume the centrality of contra-sexual relationships in the psychology of normal mature women. None of them have anything to say about the ongoing positive significance of sisterly experience as opening women toward an affirmative attitude toward their own femininity or toward deep adult relationships with same-sex others. All three were self-consciously father's daughters. Only Deutsch had sisters, both enough older than herself to make her feel that she was really an only child. Both her sisters became housewives and mothers, and Deutsch seems to have had almost no contact with them in adulthood. Though Deutsch and Horney were important pioneers as women beginning to articulate a psychology of women from a female perspective, they have less to say that stirs my soul than Freud himself. I recognize them as sisters—as unsistered sisters to whom I wish I could reveal how much women can give one another.

More involved with the analysis of actual children than Freud himself or any of the other early female analysts and, correlatively, less involved with adult patients, Melanie Klein offers us a more satisfying vision of the formative significance of early sibling experience. She maintains that even in childhood siblings are experienced as primarily inner objects. The child incorporates primary others, "feels them to be live people inside his body in the concrete way in which deep unconscious fantasies are experienced. . . . Thus an inner world is being built up in the child's unconscious mind, corresponding to his actual experiences and the impressions he gains from people and the external world, and yet altered by his own phantasies and impulses." She emphasizes, perhaps even more than Freud, the jealousy and hostility, the sadistic aggressiveness, that children feel toward their siblings—and the fear of punishment and consequent guilt that this hostility provokes. Because the hatred is so intense, it is inevitably repressed and therefore remains unconscious but operative throughout life. The hostility is directed primarily toward younger siblings, but even youngest and only children are susceptible to feeling such hostility and its consequent guilt. They feel responsible for having prevented the birth of later children, for having murdered unborn children resident in the mother's womb.

When Klein writes specifically of what a sister means to a female child, she wants us to remember we are really speaking of the internalized sister who represents a part of the self split off from the ego—either a mad, paranoid, schizoid part of the self or an idealized part of the self capable of love. The wish for reconnection to one's sister thus represents a longing to recover a lost part of one's self.

Klein believes that real siblings help enormously in enabling the child to detach from parents and to build up a new, less intense type of relationship. She believes that the sister typically replaces the mother in a boy's longing very early and sees this renunciation as the child's first experience of mourning, the first capitulation to reality. Later, other children, cousins or playmates, may appear who serve as surrogates for the sibling; these still less intense relationships are another important foundation step toward adult social relationships. However, when siblings are not available to take on the transitional role, the relationship to friends may become inappropriately intense; the imagined hostility of the unborn siblings may be projected onto unfriendly peers. The positive aspects of the missing sibling are often projected onto an imaginary companion, animal or human. Such an imaginary sibling, like an actual sibling, can help the child cope with Oedipal tensions and separate more effectively from the mother. In the more diffuse relationship to an actual or imaginary sibling it is easier to sort out love and hate than in the relationship with a parent.

(However, Klein warns, if as is often the case, there is sexual play between brother and sister—looking, touching, performing excretion in common, fellatio, cunninilingus, direct attempts at coitus—there may be intense guilt, for the child is likely to feel that the sibling love object is a substitute for mother or father. When a boy is seduced by an older sister, the threat to his assurance of his own masculinity may be enormous.)

Because the guilt or hostility directed toward siblings is less intense than that toward parents, the "drive to make reparation, which may be impeded if the feelings of guilt are over-strong, can come more fully into play." Klein is persuaded of the importance of letting the death wish toward siblings become conscious. Only thus can the guilt be relieved enough to permit the release of the love that is also felt. She emphasizes the power and persistence of this guilt, sees it evident, for example, in the faithfulness with which a little girl will nurse and bandage her doll. The guilt leads to the wish to make good, leads to a longing for reparation. Love in an active sense comes from this guilt toward the injured loved one. Such reparation is more possible with siblings than parents because the guilt is less intense. It is from our relations with siblings that we first discover our capacity to love, our urge to make others happy. Our guilt for the hostility directed against our siblings in childhood leads us to feel solicitude toward others later on, especially toward those dependent on us. Our sibling experience especially affects our parenting; we love our children to make up for our sibling guilt. Our child's vulnerability arouses our tenderness, and we give it the love we were restrained from giving a brother or sister.[4]

Klein attributes enormous significance to early sibling experience but has little to say about the distinctive aspects of *female* development or about adult psychology.

Contemporary feminist theorists influenced by Freud have, on the other hand, explored the wide-ranging lifelong effects of the fact that the earliest relation in an infant girl's life is with a same-sex other, the mother, but have almost entirely ignored the salience of sibling experience in childhood or later. After the initial angry denunciations of Freud put forward by Simone de Beauvoir and Kate Millett[5] that marked the beginning of contemporary feminism, feminists discovered resources in Freud for their own reformulations that had earlier been invisible. Juliet Mitchell's *Psychoanalysis and Feminism* provided a close reading of Freud that issued in an appreciation of the sublety of his understanding of gender formation in a father-dominated society and of his description of the developmental processes that encourage female misogyny and the consequent devaluation and distrust women so easily feel toward one another. She was especially impressed by his analysis of how deeply rooted and difficult to change these inner attitudes are.[6]

More recently feminist thinkers have moved from criticism to construction. Taking Freud's later essays on femininity and female sexuality as their starting point, they have discovered in the differences between the infantile bond between daughters and mothers and the son-mother bond the basis for a highly sophisticated psychology of gender. Much of what they see Freud also saw—but from so different a value perspective as to represent an entirely new psychology. Where Freud disparaged, they celebrate what Carol Gilligan calls "the different voice" that being raised female may make more easily accessible to women.[7]

The road that leads from Freud to these visions of an ethics that is affiliative, concrete, personal, rather than competitive and abstract, of an image of maturity that values the capacity for intimacy as highly as autonomy, is fascinating. The vision of these theorists is not a naively celebratory one, for they recognize how the intensity of that early same-sex bonding may hamper women by encouraging them to become specialists in empathy, overinvested in their own children, and restricted in their experience of those pleasures of mastery and creativity, of "world making" that alone seem to reconcile us humans to our consciousness of being separate and mortal creatures. Seeing that mother-raised daughters, though less afraid of fusion than men, are overfearful of autonomy, feminists such as Dorothy Dinnerstein and Nancy Chodorow have put their hopes on changes in patterns of parenting that would include fathers as fully equal partners.[8]

The emphasis of these Americans influenced by Freud has been almost entirely on the formative power of parent-child experience. Dinnerstein writes of how the daughter's inevitable ambivalence toward the omnipotent phallic mother of early infancy persists as a lifelong ambivalence toward women that stops us from being one another's sisters. Yet she also recognizes that girls may have a better sense of the continuity between the early mother and the later, more actual mother, and thus access to a livelier sense of compunction for her. If the split-off antagonism. toward the mother that accompanies this compunction can be recognized and integrated, it can become the basis for real solidarity among women. But her expectation is still that it is *fathers* who would help such working-through.

Some of the French feminists influenced by Freud (and by Lacan), also concerned that women must move beyond having the mother-daughter relationship intrude into all woman-woman intimacy, see the *sister* rather than the father as the figure to call upon for help. They look upon sisterly bonds as at the heart of any transformation of patriarchy—not just institutional transformations but the even more difficult inner, psychological ones.

Hélène Cixous, Luce Irigaray, Julia Kristeva, Jane Gallop[9] help us recognize how easily we move into seeing one another as mother—expect of one another the power we once attributed to her of being able to fully meet our longing to be understood, to be loved, to be taken care of—and how angrily we interpret failure as refusal.

If only, they suggest, we could see that both of us, you and I, are mother *and* daughter, that both are powerful and needy. If we could remember what we as adult women know, that the experience of motherhood is not an experience of omnipotence but of vulnerability, we would recognize in the mother a sister. They understand that it is more comforting to believe in the phallic mother—the turn to the sister is, as Freud said, a lesson in mourning and renunciation, a coming to terms with finitude and mortality. It is also a discovery of the richness of relationships based neither on fusion or identity nor on polarization but on a likeness that encompasses difference. The difference creates a space for mutual exploring, giving, support—and, of course, also for misunderstanding and failure—as the acceptance of our shared finitude creates a space for forgiveness and going on.

I find in the work of these women the beginnings of a powerful new articulation of what we as women mean when we affirm our sisterhood.

CONCLUSION

two women, eye to eye
measuring each other's spirit, each other's
limitless desire,

a whole new poetry beginning here.

—Adrienne Rich

11. Our Sisterhood

When I first came in touch with my pull to explore the meaning of sisterly relationships, I probably imagined this as primarily referring to my relationship to my actual sister—may have thought in terms of sorting through the years of shared history and working toward a deeper connection in the present. That understanding sisterhood mostly has to do with *her*, mostly has to do with fixing things, is a perspective I left behind long ago. And I do remember that even at the beginning it was not so much she as my dying sister-in-law who seemed to be calling me to this task. This meant that the point was not changing things between us but coming to appreciate how the long-established patterns of sisterly interaction enter into the primary relationships of my ongoing life. The point was also somehow connected to a coming to terms with death.

Wanting a perfect relationship with that other in the world most like oneself—one's same-sex sibling—may be an ineradicable fantasy. Yet I have come to believe that giving it up (except as fantasy) is among the deepest lessons that honest engagement with the meaning of this relationship has to teach: That relationships aren't perfect. That the sister so like me is *other*. That the particular, subtle, inexpungible ways in which we are intimate and distant, alike and different, are precisely what our sisterhood is all about. Coming to accept that we are not identical and won't be, that our differences don't add up to make one beautifully balanced whole, that somehow they aren't the "right" differences for that seems to be part of what we come to discover and accept. In a sense we always have the wrong sister—and that's just what makes her right, just what makes us aware of the reality of otherness, of what is involved in seeing another as other, in letting her be herself. It may also be just how she helps me discover who I really am.

In the beginning, we seem to look to our sister to fulfill a longing for another just like ourselves, as we look to our mother to fulfill a longing to dissolve all otherness. We end by discovering in our relation to our sister what is required of us in accepting that she truly is *another*. I have been signally aware of a particular dimension of that acceptance throughout the composition of this book. My own sister is not comfortable with the degree of self-disclosure I risked in my book on the Greek goddesses. Honoring her sense of privacy has meant that this book had to be written in a different way.

This is at the heart of what I have learned from Psyche and her sisters—that, though not the sisters she would have chosen, they are *her* sisters, the ones that start her on the journey to herself.

Wanting to change the relationship, to fix it, to deepen it, to make it more central in our lives is often, I've come to believe, really wanting to change her, to be in control, to make her part of me. Jung helps us to understand that this is a misplaced longing, that what it really signifies is a longing to change myself, to claim as my own aspects of my own potentiality that I long ago saw as belonging to her rather than to myself. The "deidentification" that was appropriate in childhood becomes anachronistic; we do not forever have to divide the world into her sphere and my sphere.

It seems that one of the dimensions on which such polarization often occurs is precisely that of intimacy; one sister wants more, the other resists her attempts as invasive. So often one sister wants the relationship to be different, better, more intense; but when she says, "I want to know you better," the other replies, "That just shows you don't want to know *me!*" Paradoxically, backing off, communicating, "I no longer want to change you, no longer need you to be 'my' sister," can sometimes open the way to a more spontaneously flowing, mutually enjoyable relationship.

But I have come to believe that we don't really want the "fixing" anyway, that that's a surrogate for something else. I've certainly discovered that sisters matter terribly to adult women, that the relationship feels focal, vital, often painful—and most especially *untold*. Whenever I have mentioned my interest in sisters, even casually, women have wanted to tell me their story—

urgently, fully, intimately—often as though they had never before realized how *much* they wanted to tell it.

Like Helen and Klytemnestra, many of us seem to believe that to tell our own stories well, to tell you how I became who I am, involves telling you about my sister. We want to relate our particular story, which feels unique and unfinished. It is as though the one who listens to the narrative unfolding provides the confirmation we might once have looked for from the sister herself. Perhaps what we most deeply want is simply to have this story about ourselves and our sisters heard—and blessed. Perhaps we don't really want to be part of a different story at all.

Sisterhood and story telling seem to be closely intertwined. Perhaps that is why the mortal heroines of Greek mythology who became themselves in their stories, their histories, were sistered, as the goddesses who are always already themselves were not. I remember how my own story telling began as I told stories to the sister in the bed across the room, stories that were always in a sense about us. I recall, too, Thomas Mann inviting us to his feast of story telling, and I see the central part of this book as such a feast, an anthology of sibling stories that communicate the great variety of ways in which brotherhood and sisterhood have been lived and understood.

When we seize the chance to tell our story, we seem to know that its beauty and power comes from its being *our* story, a never-before-told story. We are released from the illusion that there is one right version of the story, one normative pattern of sisterly experience, to which ours should conform. We take it for granted that there are many different patterns, each with its own pains, its own gifts.

It has been important for me to see clearly the shape of my relationship with my sister, as it was in childhood and as it is now. To acknowledge on what a low key it is mostly lived, how rarely we spend time together that is not shared with other family members, how evident it is that we are more intimate with others than with each other—but also how utterly we can trust that the other will be there in moments of crisis, emotionally as well as practically. I marvel at how different our bond is from that between my lover and her older sister. Their's is a relationship so intense, so permeated with a sense of deeply entangled destinies, that it seems to require long periods of total separation. The very intensity seems almost to preclude any day-by-day outward intimacy. Two very different stories, two good stories—"good" in the sense that stories are good, rich, full, complicated, still alive and changing, not "good" in the sense of easy or success-filled.

"Good" also in the sense that the other stories included in the book are good stories—good stories to know: stories in which we recognize ourselves at the same time that we realize these are not the only stories, just a sampling, just a beginning. But to become aware of the rich kaleidoscope of sisterly experience is also to see that we are not necessarily limited to living only the story we have already lived. Telling a story about sisters well discloses how the sisters co-create each other. With another woman I can sister differently than I sistered in the past—and can allow myself to be sistered differently. It helps to know lots of stories.

Attending to the stories brings into view the uniqueness of sisterly relationships, how they differ both from relationships among brothers and from those between sisters and brothers. It also helps clarify how the early bond between daughter and mother contributes to the special closeness that sisters may have with one another but may also complicate their bond.

Relationships between sisters seem to be more intense and emotionally intimate than between brothers, which means that it may also be harder for us to tolerate differences without experiencing them as betrayal. The myths and fairy tales represent brothers as engaging together in adventures in the outer world, whereas sisters share feelings and inner experience. My sense is that our sisterhood might be strengthened were we to incorporate some more "brotherly" support of one another, were we to commit ourselves to arousing one another to the full exercise of our powers in the world, the outer world of work and creativity. But the "heart" of sisterhood is truly different from this fraternal kind of bonding.

The tales about sister-brother relationships suggest the deep meaning this bond has in the inner lives of men; "sister" seems to signify that which connects them to the realm of feeling, to their own inner depths, their soul, and what enables them to turn trustingly toward death. The sister represents a relation to what men seem truly to experience as their own inner but often inaccessible and mysterious "femininity"—a relation to that femininity that is life-bringing rather than death-dealing, less frightening than the otherness represented by the mother. For men this contra-sexual relationship carries tremendous power. For women, the brother, the contra-sexual other, seems to mean less than the same-sex other, the sister.

For us, too, the sister carries the soul-meaning that the sister carries for men. For us, too, she embodies that same connection to the source of our lives, the source of meaning, that the mother originally embodies—but less fearfully. Relationships among women seem inevitably to recall our relationships to our mother; the intensity, the intimacy, that are often so easily available to us confirm that. This is the source of both the strength and the fragility of sisterly bonds. Fusion longing, fusion fear, almost inevitably appear—to enrich and complicate. We look to one another for all-giving nurturance and are angry when we get too little—or too much.

I see "sisterhood" as the right name for close relationships among adult women because it communicates a real intimacy that is based on an early experience of mutual giving and receiving. The actual sisters of childhood are in some sense our first mother surrogates, but we never expected from them the absolute love that at first we associate with our mothers. To speak of later women intimates as "sisters" is to acknowledge that this process of substitution goes on, that the point was never to remain forever within the original constellation. Coming to understand the meaning of sisterhood means learning about what happens in families and how this is passed down from one generation to the next—and how it is passed from the familial relationships of childhood into the relationships we form as adults.

If we can remember that we are here to sister one another, not to mother or be mothered, the possibility of another kind of relationship is opened to us. The turn from mothers to sisters is, as Freud saw, like the turn from goddesses to human women, the transition from a sacred to a profane relationship. Between sisters there is the possibility of a genuinely mutual, reciprocal relationship; each is giver and receiver. We can know the other as a flawed and needy human woman—like ourselves. When we do not expect her to be able to answer all our needs, to be all-good, we do not feel betrayed when she does not and is not. The moments of fusion when they occur can be celebrated—because we know they are *moments*, transformative but evanescent. We remember how intensely ambivalent and volatile those early interactions with our actual sister may have been and are not terrified when closeness temporarily disappears, when unexpected differences are suddenly revealed.

Though we may not be "blood" sisters, may not literally be born of the same womb, I believe women may discover their sisteredness to be just as much a *given* in their lives. What a gift to know that a relationship will endure despite its ebbing and flowing, despite times when the other's otherness leaves us feeling unbearably alone. Recollection of early sisterly experience reminds us that relationships have their dark side—and that this is part of what makes them life-giving, transformative. There is space within sisterhood for likeness and difference, for the subtle differences that challenge and delight; there is space for disappointment—and surprise.

That real acceptance of otherness that Thomas Mann took to be the point of brotherly experience and that I see as such a central element in what I mean by sisterhood leads also to a new understanding of self. Sisters teach us our limits—teach us that we are contingent, finite, and mortal beings. Sisters teach us that someday we will die—and that that is simply part of having been here at all. Over and over as I reflect on my own experience and on the many myths of sisterhood I discover again this intertwining of the two themes—sisterhood and death. I have come to see death as a mystery like childbirth, a women's mystery. There is a Käthe Kollwitz drawing of Death with a woman in her lap: I see Death and the dying woman as sisters.

Sisterhood—the deeply intimate interdependent relationship between women that sustains us even as we fail one another—has become a model for me of relationships in so many arenas of my life where I find the parent-child model oppressive and misleading: in my roles as teacher and therapist, in my friendships, in my bonds with my adult children, in my primary bond with my lover.

I have come to see it as also relevant to our understanding of our relationship to the natural world. Seeing the earth as Mother ignores our responsibility to it, our interdependence with all that lives, and encourages a sentimental hope that somehow no matter what we humans do, She will forgive, everything will be all right. To be able to say instead, as Susan Griffin does, "This earth is my *sister*,"[1] is to affirm a more mutual connection. To recognize in the other creatures that share this planet with us, brothers and sisters, is to acknowledge our shared finitude, our shared danger. Reflection on sisterhood has led me to discover my real connection to all the particular other beings among whom I live:

> I do not mean *the earth*. I mean the
> earth that is here and browns your
> feet, thickens your fingers,
> unfurls in your brain and in
> these onion seedlings
> I set in flats, lovingly under
> a spare window
>
> There is no *other*.[2]

As I bring this exploration of sisterhood to a close the image that comes to me is that of the tender awe with which my twenty-month-old granddaughter looks upon her twenty-day-old sister: A whole new poetry beginning here . . .

Notes

INTRODUCTION

Adrienne Rich, "Sibling Mysteries," *The Dream of a Common Language* (New York: W. W. Norton, 1978), p. 51.

CHAPTER ONE: THE MYSTERIES OF SISTERHOOD

1. Christine Downing, *The Goddess: Mythological Images of the Feminine* (New York: Crossroad, 1981).
2. Adrienne Rich, "Sibling Mysteries," *The Dream of a Common Language* (New York: W. W. Norton, 1978), pp. 50f.
3. Rich, "Sibling Mysteries," p. 58.
4. Carl Kerenyi, *The Heroes of the Greeks* (New York: Grove Press, 1962), p. 13.
5. For the former, cf. Toni A. H. McNaron, *The Sister Bond* (New York: Pergamon Press, 1985); for the latter, Louise Bernikow, "Sisters," *Among Women* (New York: Harper & Row, 1980), pp. 73–109.

PART I: MYTHOLOGY'S SISTERS

Adrienne Rich, "Transit," *The Fact of a Doorframe* (New York: W. W. Norton, 1984), pp. 283f.

CHAPTER TWO: FAIRY-TALE SISTERS

1. Sigmund Freud, "From the History of an Infantile Neurosis," *The Standard Edition of the Complete Psychological Works of Sigmund Freud,* vol. 17 (London: Hogarth Press, 1981), pp. 3–122. Cf. also Freud, "The Occurrence in Dreams of Material from Fairytales," *Standard Edition,* vol. 12, pp. 279–87.
2. Thomas Mann, "Freud and the Future," *Essays of Three Decades* (New York: Alfred A. Knopf, 1971), p. 422.
3. Jacob Grimm, *Teutonic Mythology,* vol. 1 (New York: Dover, 1966), p. 8.
4. Cf. J. R. R. Tolkien, "On Fairy-Stories," in *Essays Presented*

to Charles Williams (Grand Rapids: William R. Eerdmans, 1966), pp. 38–89; and David L. Miller, "Fairytale or Myth," *Spring* 1976, pp. 157–64.

5. In addition to the two essays cited above, cf. Marie Louise von Franz, *Problems of the Feminine in Fairytales* (Irving, TX: Spring Publications, 1972); and Bruno Bettelheim, *The Uses of Enchantment* (New York: Alfred A. Knopf, 1976).

6. Cf. Colette Dowling, *The Cinderella Complex* (New York: Summit, 1981).

7. Geza Roheim, *Psychoanalysis and Anthropology* (New York: International Universities Press, 1968), p. 468.

8. Tolkien, "On Fairy-Stories," p. 81.

9. von Franz, *Feminine in Fairytales*, pp. 114–42.

10. Sigmund Freud, "The Theme of the Three Caskets," *S.E.*, vol. 12, pp. 295f.

11. Grimm, *Mythology*, vol. 4, pp. 1367, 1545, 1588–91.

12. Bettelheim, *Enchantment*, pp. 274ff.

13. von Franz, *Feminine in Fairytales*, p. 57.

CHAPTER THREE: PSYCHE AND HER SISTERS

1. I follow the convention of using the Greek names for the god and goddess in my discussion rather than the Roman ones employed by Apuleius.

2. Marie Louise von Franz, *A Psychological Interpretation of the Golden Ass of Apuleius* (Dallas, TX: Spring Publications, 1980), pp. 63ff.

3. Erich Neumann, *Amor and Psyche: The Psychic Development of the Feminine* (New York: Harper & Row, 1962), p. 81.

4. Cf. Erwin Rohde, *Psyche* (New York: Harper & Row, 1966); R. B. Onions, *The Origins of European Thought* (Cambridge: Cambridge University Press, 1954), pp. 472–76.

5. Freud, "Three Caskets," *S.E.*, vol. 12, p. 293.

6. Robert A. Johnson, *She* (King of Prussia, PA: Religious Publishing, 1976), p. 29.

7. J. J. Bachofen, *Myth, Religion and Mother Right* (Princeton: Princeton University Press, 1973), p. 45.

8. James Hillman, *The Myth of Analysis* (Evanston: Northwestern University Press, 1972), p. 58.

9. C. S. Lewis, *Till We Have Faces* (Grand Rapids: William B. Eerdmans, 1966).
10. Neumann, *Amor and Psyche*, pp. 72ff.
11. Rainer Maria Rilke, "Orpheus, Eurydice, Hermes," in Stephen Mitchell, ed. and trans., *The Selected Poetry of Rainer Maria Rilke* (New York: Random House, 1982), p. 51.

CHAPTER FOUR: MYTHIC SIBLINGS

1. George Steiner, *Antigones* (New York: Oxford University Press, 1984), p. 121.
2. Lewis Richard Farnell, *Greek Hero Cults and Ideas of Immortality* (Oxford: Oxford University Press, 1921), p. 358.
3. The quote from Euripides' *The Medea* (lines 416–431) is taken from an essay by Bernard Knox, "The Medea of Euripides," in Erich Segal, ed., *Greek Tragedy* (New York: Harper & Row, 1983), p. 291.
4. Gregory Nagy, *The Best of the Achaeans* (Baltimore: Johns Hopkins, 1979), p. 9.
5. Aeschylus, *Seven Against Thebes* (lines 689f., 703f.), trans. David Grene, in David Grene and Richmond Lattimore, eds., *Aeschylus* (Chicago: University of Chicago Press, 1959), p. 286.
6. Edward Tripp, *Classical Mythology* (New York: Thomas Y. Crowell, 1970), p. 362.
7. Knox, "The Medea," p. 292.
8. Sophokles, *Electra* (lines 1146f., 1232), trans. David Grene, in David Grene and Richmond Lattimore, eds., *Sophocles* (Chicago: University of Chicago Press, 1959), pp. 376, 381.
9. Euripides, *Orestes* (lines 616–623), trans. William Arrowsmith, in David Grene and Richmond Lattimore, eds., *Euripides* (Chicago: University of Chicago Press, 1960), vol. 4, pp. 227f.
10. Steiner, *Antigones*, p. 17 and *passim*.

CHAPTER FIVE: TRAGIC SISTERS

1. Karl Kerenyi, *Goddesses of Sun and Moon* (Irving, TX: Spring Publications, 1979), pp. 1–19.
2. Cf. Christine Downing, "Ariadne: Mistress of the Labyrinth," *Goddess*.

3. Mary Renault, *The Bull from the Sea* (New York: Pocket Books, 1963).

4. Boris Matthews, trans., *The Herder Symbol Dictionary* (Wilmette, IL: 1986), pp. 138, 188.

5. Adrienne Rich, "To Judith Taking Leave," *The Fact of a Doorframe*, p. 193f.

6. Steiner, *Antigones*, pp. 209ff.; Robert Fagles, trans., *The Three Theban Plays of Sophocles* (New York: Viking, 1982), p. 41; R. E. Braun, trans., *Sophocles' Antigone* (New York: Oxford University Press, 1973), p. 21.

7. Linda Lee Clader, *Helen: The Evolution from Divine to Heroic in Greek Epic Tradition* (Lugoluni Batavorum: Brill, 1976).

8. E. A. S. Butterworth, *Some Traces of the Pre-Olympian World* (Berlin: DeGruyter, 1966).

9. R. P. Winnington-Ingram, "Clytemnestra and the Vote of Athena," in Segal, ed., *Greek Tragedy*, pp. 100–103.

10. Cf. Christa Wolf, *Cassandra* (New York: Farrar, Straus, Giroux, 1984).

11. Aeschylus, *Agamemnon* (lines 1456–1466), trans. Richmond Lattimore, in David Grene and Richmond Lattimore, eds., *Aeschylus* (Chicago: University of Chicago Press, 1959), pp. 82f.

CHAPTER SIX: DIVINE SISTERS—AND BIBLICAL BROTHERS

1. Merlin Stone, *When God Was a Woman* (New York: Harcourt Brace Jovanovich, 1976); Gerda Lerner, *The Creation of Patriarchy* (New York: Oxford University Press, 1986).

2. Sylvia Brington Perera, *Descent to the Goddess* (Toronto: Inner City, 1981); Diane Wolkstein and Samuel Noah Kramer, *Inanna* (New York: Harper & Row, 1983); Betty DeShong Meador's translation of the Inanna myth will appear in Judy Grahn, *Queen of Swords* (Boston: Beacon Press, forthcoming).

3. Perera, *Descent*, p. 7.

4. Friedrich Solmsen, *Isis Among the Greeks and Romans* (Cambridge: Harvard University Press, 1979).

5. Erik Hornung, *Conceptions of God in Ancient Egypt* (London: Routledge & Kegan Paul, 1893).

6. J. A. Philips, *Eve* (San Francisco: Harper & Row, 1984).

7. Thomas Mann, *Joseph and His Brothers* (New York: Alfred A. Knopf, 1983).
8. Mann, "Freud," *Essays*, pp. 422f.
9. Mann, *Joseph*, p. 1207.

PART TWO: PSYCHOLOGY'S SISTERS

Adrienne Rich, "A Woman Dead in Her Forties," *Dream of a Common Language*, p. 56.

CHAPTER SEVEN: RESEARCHING SIBLINGS

1. Heinz L. Ansbacher and Rowena R. Ansbacher, eds. *The Individual Psychology of Alfred Adler* (New York: Harper & Row, 1964), pp. 63, 80, 115, and *passim*. For a "depth" reading of Adler, cf. James Hillman, "What Does the Soul Want?: Adler's Imagination of Inferiority," *Healing Fiction* (Barrytown, NY: Station Hill Press, 1983), pp. 83–130.
2. Ansbacher and Ansbacher, *Adler*, pp. 376ff.
3. Ibid., pp. 40, 113ff., 133ff., and *passim*.
4. Ibid., p. 155.
5. Brian Sutton-Smith and B. G. Rosenberg, *The Sibling* (New York: Holt, Rinehart & Winston, 1970); Michael Lamb and Brian Sutton-Smith, eds., *Sibling Relationships: Their Nature and Significance Across the Life Span* (Hillsdale, NJ: Lawrence Erlbaum Associates, 1982); Stephen P. Bank and Michael D. Kahn, *The Sibling Bond* (New York: Basic Books, 1982); Judy Dunn and Carol Kendrick, *Siblings: Love, Envy and Understanding* (Cambridge: Harvard University Press, 1982).
6. Victor C. Cicirelli, "Sibling Influence Throughout the LifeSpan," in Lamb and Sutton-Smith, *Sibling Relationships*, p. 269.
7. Thomas S. Weisner, "Sibling Interdependence and Child Care-Taking: A Crosscultural View," in Lamb and Sutton-Smith, *Sibling Relationships*, pp. 395–27.
8. Sutton-Smith and Rosenberg, *Sibling*, pp. 142–55.
9. Frances Ruchs Schachter, "Sibling Deidentification and Split-Parent Identification," in Lamb and Sutton-Smith, *Sibling Relationships*, p. 133.

10. Walter Toman, *The Family Constellation* (New York: Springer, 1961).
11. John Bowlby, *Attachment* (New York: Basic Books, 1982), p. 119.
12. Dunn and Kendrick, *Siblings,* pp. 86–159; Rona Abramovitch, Debra Pepler, and Carl Corter, "Patterns of Sibling Interaction Among Preschool Children," in Lamb and Sutton-Smith, *Sibling Relationships,* p. 84.

CHAPTER EIGHT: INNER SISTERS

1. William McGuire, ed., *The Freud/Jung Letters* (Princeton: Princeton University Press, 1974), pp. 199f.
2. C. G. Jung, "Archetypes of the Collective Unconscious," *Collected Works,* vol. 9.1 (New York: Pantheon, 1959), p. 4.
3. C. G. Jung, "Concerning the Archetypes and the Anima Concept," *C.W.,* vol. 9.1, p. 70.
4. C. G. Jung, "On the Nature of the Psyche," *C.W.,* vol. 8, pp. 208, 346.
5. C. G. Jung, "Symbols of the Mother and Rebirth," *C.W.,* vol. 5, p. 259; C. G. Jung, *Two Essays on Analytical Psychology, C.W.* vol. 7, pp. 38, 75.
6. C. G. Jung, "Concerning Rebirth," *C.W.,* vol. 9.1, p. 131.
7. Otto Rank, *The Double* (Chapel Hill: University of North Carolina Press, 1971); *Beyond Psychology* (New York: Dover, 1941).
8. C. G. Jung, "Analytical Psychology and Education," *C.W.,* vol. 17, pp. 129–31.
9. C. G. Jung, "Individual Dream Symbolism in Relation to Alchemy," *C.W.,* vol. 12, pp. 69f.
10. C. G. Jung, *Mysterium Coniunctionis, C.W.,* vol. 14, pp. 91f.
11. Demaris Wehr, "Uses and Abuses of Jung's Animus Theory," *Anima,* Fall 1985, pp. 13–22.
12. Irene Claremont de Castillejo, *Knowing Woman* (New York: Harper & Row, 1973), pp. 165–82.
13. C. G. Jung, "The Psychological Aspects of the Kore," *C.W.,* vol. 9.1, pp. 182–203.
14. M. Esther Harding. *The Way of All Women* (New York: Harper & Row, 1975), pp. 273f., 289.
15. Hillman, *Myth,* p. 58.

16. Jung, *Mysterium*, p. 470.
17. James Hillman, "Senex and Puer," *The Puer Papers* (Dallas, TX: Spring, 1979), pp. 3–30.
18. Patricia Berry, "The Training of Shadow and the Shadow of Training," *Echo's Subtle Body* (Dallas, TX: Spring, 1982), pp. 187–98.
19. James Hillman, *Anima* (Dallas, TX: Spring, 1985), especially pp. 51–69.

CHAPTER NINE: OEDIPUS' SISTERS

1. Steiner, *Antigones*, p. 6.
2. Sigmund Freud, *The Interpretation of Dreams*, S.E., vol. 4, pp. 261f.
3. Ernest L. Freud, *The Letters of Sigmund Freud* (New York: Basic Books, 1960), p. 382.
4. Sigmund Freud, "Femininity," *New Introductory Lectures*, S.E., vol. 22, pp. 112–36.
5. Sigmund Freud, *Three Essays on Sexuality*, S.E., vol. 7, p. 226.
6. Sigmund Freud, *Introductory Lectures on PsychoAnalysis*, S.E., vol. 15, p. 153.
7. Sigmund Freud, "A Childhood Recollection from *Dictung und Wahrheit*," S.E., vol. 7, pp. 145–56.
8. Sigmund Freud, "The Sexual Enlightenment of Children," S.E., vol. 9, pp. 129–34.
9. Sigmund Freud, "Family Romances," S.E., vol. 9, pp. 237–41.
10. Sigmund Freud, *Introductory Lectures*, S.E., vol. 15, p. 204.
11. Ibid., p. 205.
12. Sigmund Freud, *Group Psychology and the Analysis of the Ego*, S.E., vol. 18, p. 120.
13. Sigmund Freud, *Totem and Taboo*, S.E., vol. 13, pp. 141ff.
14. Sigmund Freud, *Group Psychology*, S.E., vol. 18, p. 141.
15. Sigmund Freud, "Some Psychichal Consequences of the Anatomical Distinction Between the Sexes," S.E., vol. 19, pp. 248–58.
16. Sigmund Freud, *Five Lectures*, S.E., vol. 5, p. 48.
17. Sigmund Freud, "Three Caskets," S.E., vol. 12, pp. 293f.
18. H. D. (Hilda Doolittle), *Tribute to Freud* (New York: McGraw-Hill, 1974), p. 47.

19. Lucy Freeman and Herbert Stream, *Freud and Women* (New York: Frederick Ungar, 1981).

CHAPTER TEN: FEMINISM'S SISTERS

1. Helene Deutsch, *The Psychology of Women* (New York: Bantam, 1973), pp. 26–152.
2. Clara Thompson, *On Women* (New York: New American Library, 1971), pp. 44, 59.
3. Karen Horney, *Feminine Psychology* (New York: W. W. Norton, 1967), pp. 163–244.
4. Sibling experience is a pervasive and major theme throughout Klein's writing; cf. Melanie Klein, *Contributions to Psychoanalysis* (London: Hogarth Press, 1968); *Envy and Gratitude* (New York: Delacorte, 1975); *Love, Guilt and Reparation* (New York: Delacorte, 1975).
5. Simone de Beauvoir, *The Second Sex* (New York: Bantam, 1961), pp. 33–47; Kate Millett, *Sexual Politics* (New York: Doubleday, 1970), pp. 176–202.
6. Juliet Mitchell, *Psychoanalysis and Feminism* (New York: Random House, 1974).
7. Carol Gilligan, *In a Different Voice* (Cambridge: Harvard University Press, 1982); Jean Baker Miller, *Toward a New Psychology of Women* (Boston: Beacon Press, 1976).
8. Dorothy Dinnerstein, *The Mermaid and the Minotaur* (New York: Harper & Row, 1977); Nancy Chodorov, *The Reproduction of Mothering* (Berkeley: University of California Press, 1978).
9. The best introduction to these difficult-to-translate and sometimes difficult-to-understand-in-translation French thinkers is Jane Gallop, *The Daughter's Seduction* (Ithaca: Cornell University Press, 1982). Most of the ideas I summarize are discussed on pp. 113–31; her bibliography is excellent, although by now more of the primary work is available in English.

CONCLUSION

Adrienne Rich, "Transcendental Etude," *Dream of a Common Language*, p. 76.

CHAPTER ELEVEN: OUR SISTERHOOD

1 Susan Griffin, *Woman and Nature: The Roaring Inside Her* (New York: Harper & Row, 1982), p. 18, my emphasis.

2. Margaret Atwood, *Two-Headed Poems* (Toronto: Oxford University Press, 1978), pp. 96f. I am indebted to Estella Lauter for introducing me to this poem. The final chapter of her book, *Women as Mythmaker* (Bloomington: Indiana University Press, 1984), expresses an awareness of the importance of moving beyond mother imagery for the natural world that is very close to the view I am presenting here.

Index